Praise for
The Leader They Want

"*In the new book,* The Leader They Want, *Scott clearly makes the case as to why leadership is a key component to a business's overall success or demise. He takes real-time feedback and shares several ways for any organization to improve their leadership, but more importantly build a deeper connection with their team. Get this book. Read it, apply its wisdom, and reap the many positive benefits you will see materialize within your organization. Well done, Scott! Thanks for this timely and important book.*"

—**Tony Rubleski**, Bestselling Author
of the *Mind Capture* Book Series
MindCaptureGroup.com

"The Leader They Want *really breaks down the best ways to lead your people. As a CEO and leader of my company, I can see using the action steps at the end of each chapter to improve the way I currently lead to better inspire others. I have known Scott for many years and truly appreciate the way he teaches, and this book is more proof of that.*"

—**Katie Lance**, CEO/Founder,
Katie Lance Consulting

"The Leader They Want, *Scott Comey's most recent book*, *offers a wide range of leadership concepts from successful leaders and their workers from different industries. His book is brimming with insightful information and guidance for all leaders. To motivate us to become better people and leaders, Scott uses examples from his more than thirty years of experience as a leader and mentor. For leaders who wish to prioritize their team members and create a culture of service-based leadership, this book is essential reading. Thank you, Scott, for sharing your knowledge with his great leadership book."*

—**Greg Kettner**, TedX Speaker
& Founder at WorkHappy
Gregkettner.com

"Scott Comey's The Leader They Want *nails what it takes to be the kind of leader people genuinely want to follow. As a former CEO, I learned how crucial empathy, authenticity, and clear communication are in leadership, and Scott captures these perfectly. If you're looking to step up your leadership game, this book is a must-read."*

—**Adam Contos**,
Former CEO of RE/MAX LLC
adamcontos.com

"Scott showcases a great blend of different perspectives on leadership from people across various industries. If you are currently leading a team, another individual, or even an entire company, this book can help you become a more inspiring leader."

—**Brian Moran**, CEO & Founder
of 12 Week Year, NY Times Bestselling Author
12weekyear.com

"Scott Comey's, The Leader They Want *is a game-changer for anyone looking to provide real impact through leadership. Full of authentic, relatable stories and practical, tangible advice, Comey shows us that great leadership is about connection, empathy, and empowerment. Whether you're just starting out or have been in leadership for years, this book will help you discover opportunities for personal growth and provide the tools to make a meaningful difference."*

—**Amy Somerville**,
CEO of Success Magazine & Media
success.com

THE
LEADER
THEY
WANT

Inspire and Lead through
Learning from Those You Lead

SCOTT COMEY

The Leader They Want
Copyright © 2024 by Scott Comey

Design & Distribution by Bublish, Inc.

ISBN: 978-1-64704-881-5 (eBook)
ISBN: 978-1-64704-879-2 (Paperback)
ISBN: 978-1-64704-880-8 (Hardcover)

I wish to dedicate this book to the best leader I know, my wife, Renee. She is a living example of what leadership should be. She is inspiring, encouraging, and a champion of mine. No one roots for me harder than she does. She is extremely smart, and I am so proud of all that she has done in her life. She continues to be the reason I have success in life. Thank you, my love, for all that you do and for putting up with me all of these years.

CONTENTS

INTRODUCTION

> If your actions create a legacy that inspires others to dream more, learn more, do more and become more, then, you are an excellent leader.
>
> —Dolly Parton

I want you to think about all of the bosses you've ever had. You've likely had some great ones and some not-so-great ones. Let's focus on each individually. What was it about the not-so-great ones that made you cringe? What did they do that frustrated you? Or maybe, what didn't they do? These are questions we must ask ourselves if we are going to fully understand how to be great leaders for our people. It starts with understanding their perspective.

There also have likely been some great bosses you respected and really liked. What characteristics did they offer that made you favor them? How did they manage you? What were the things you enjoyed about their leadership style? It's only after answering these questions that we can fully understand the way people want to be led.

In my first leadership book in the series, *Are You a Manager or a Leader?*, I interviewed several great leaders and got their take on what it means to be a great manager. I was able to hear things such as leaders tell the truth, look in the mirror, and are never content. Each of these are chapters in that book and offer great insight into the way several top leaders have led successfully over the years. The book was a great success, making it to Amazon new release bestseller status in an extremely tough category: leadership. If you haven't checked out this book, I encourage you to pick up a copy and read the stories I shared and experiences from others that have helped them become great leaders at their place of employment and businesses. That first book was a great collaboration of top leaders, CEOs, and executives from large and small companies alike. In addition, I shared many insights on leadership from my time in the military, to my time as CEO of a large real estate brokerage, to being chairman of the board for nonprofits. In fact, my leadership experience entails about thirty years of managing and leading people, and my best stuff is shared both in that book and this one.

Why a second book then, you might ask? I have been asked by several people to add more content and more stories to that first leadership book. They essentially wanted me to just come out with a revised edition.

To start that journey, I decided to post on my Facebook page a simple question: "What makes a great leader?" I was blown away by the responses of so many folks who wanted to chime in on what they felt made a great leader. Some of the responses were things never mentioned in my first book. This had me question whether a revised edition of that book was still the direction I should go. After talking with my distributor,

I opted to go a completely different route this time. What if, instead of revising a book on leadership from a leader's point of view, I wrote a book where the content and ideas mostly came from those who are being led? This was an eye-opening concept, one that excited me. I almost feel like I had it wrong the first time. A leadership book should really come from the ideas of our people. Let's give them a voice. Obviously, there are limits to sharing all of their thoughts on the subject, but how much happier would your people be if they felt like you cared about them more? What would the retention of your staff and salespeople look like if you decided not to guess what to do to keep them, but instead asked them what they look for in leadership and their relationship to the company?

That is what you now have in your hands. A book on leadership that truly will help you retain employees, create better work environments, and inspire others to want to be led by you and your team.

Looking back, one of my favorite managers was Robert from my days as a general manager at a flagship location for a franchise coffee shop. Robert seemed like he always was excited to see you. He also seemed to care about you and your family, always asking questions about that part of my life. He knew his numbers and still set proper expectations, and for that I respected him. He was not a micromanager and allowed some flexibility in how I ran my store and my people. You see, even in my simple explanation of this one leader in my life, I share why *I* appreciated him and wanted to do well by him. I wanted to make him proud. I wanted to help make his team one of the best in the country. Yet flip the coin for a minute. Robert might answer the question differently when asked what he believes makes a great leader. He may say something like, "Know your numbers, always look to grow, set proper boundaries," or similar. And yes, these elements are needed, but are they the most important when becoming the best leader you can be? That's what we will answer in this book.

It is not easy managing people. It's even more challenging when you are leading people. (There is a difference, and I explained it in my prior book.) It's time to become better. We are all capable of it. Leadership does not require a four-year degree or an MBA. It can be a learned skill, and it can be accomplished more quickly when we take into consideration our people's point of view.

One of the initial questions in my survey was, "Why did you quit your last job?" I asked them to list the reasons and give details as well. This was incredibly insightful, as many of you might be a bit shocked by the results. I think as leaders we tend to draw our own conclusions as to why people leave. I know many companies do an exit survey when people leave so that they can better understand why and possibly course correct moving forward in an effort to keep turnover down. Here are the results from the survey:

Why do people leave their jobs?

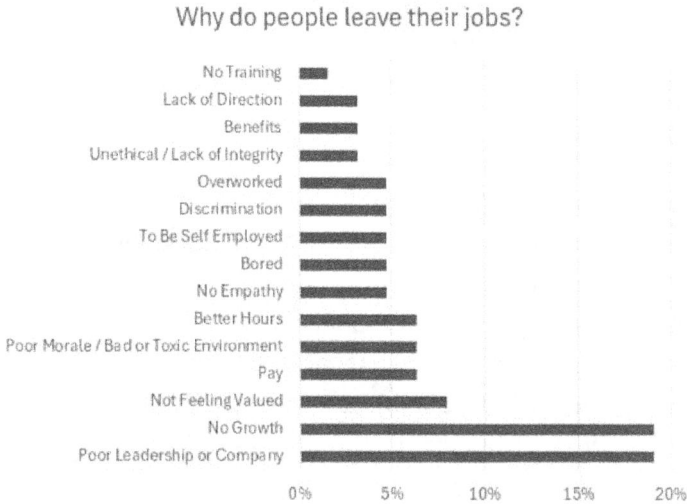

No Training	
Lack of Direction	
Benefits	
Unethical / Lack of Integrity	
Overworked	
Discrimination	
To Be Self Employed	
Bored	
No Empathy	
Better Hours	
Poor Morale / Bad or Toxic Environment	
Pay	
Not Feeling Valued	
No Growth	
Poor Leadership or Company	

0%   5%   10%   15%   20%

*Independent survey conducted 7/2024 by Turn the Dial Coaching, LLC

As you can see, the top two reasons why people leave their jobs are "poor leadership" and "no growth opportunities." We will address how to help correct these two things within your organization later in this book. But what I wanted you to see, before getting too far in, is that our perceptions of why people leave may differ from the actual reasons. If almost one out of five people state poor leadership as their reason, we cannot allow this to happen. Our leadership needs to be looked at. What can we do to fix it? Don't worry—that's why you've got this book.

The approach in this book is to ask those exact kinds of questions. What if we ask those same people what could've been done differently to keep their job? Or, for those who haven't quit their current jobs, why do they stay?

As a business owner, I've always wanted to know what my people thought of me, my company, and how we run things.

I would ask them questions like, "What's most important to you and your job with us?" and "What can we do differently that we aren't currently doing?" The answers I would get would sometimes surprise me. We don't know exactly what our employees are thinking, but by sending out regular surveys, we can gain some valuable insight.

You may be wondering how I sent these out. There are several survey companies, but I like using SurveyMonkey. It is very user friendly, and you can analyze results quickly. I would use the data collected in these surveys to share in leadership meetings and with other key staff. If something was broken, we fixed it quickly. I highly encourage you and your company to start sending surveys to your staff to see if it shows any holes in your current systems and processes.

So now you've got a taste of how this book has come to light. I am proud of what this book has become. I am also incredibly grateful for the people who have shared their thoughts on leadership to make it a book not just written by me but, with the help of several individuals from around the world, by many. I recognize everyone in the acknowledgements of this book.

My goal with this book is that no matter what level of leadership journey you are on, you will garner some golden nuggets of wisdom to implement immediately into your workplace so you can start being the best leader, one your people need and desire.

CHAPTER 1

Be One of Them

> Example is not the main thing in influencing others, it is the *only* thing.
>
> —Albert Schweitzer

Oftentimes we grew into or were promoted into a leadership position at our companies for doing a great job in a lower-level position. It is an honor to take that next step and start climbing the ladder, and it's a tilt of the cap for doing a job well done in your prior role. This chapter embodies one of the top things I heard in my several social media surveys about what people look for in their leader. You've likely been in their shoes already, and this chapter will give you great cause to not be afraid to get back in those shoes on occasion.

I truly enjoyed researching how people want to be led, and though it didn't surprise me that "lead by example" was on the list of ways our people want to be led, it did surprise me that it was at the top. It turns out workers want to see us walk the walk and not just talk the talk. It makes perfect sense. No one likes to be told what to do, and they certainly don't want to feel less than, so when a leader rolls up their sleeves and does a task normally done by their staff and employees, it is taken with great respect.

Roland Tiangco is the creative director and UX manager at eBay, and he has an awesome quote: "The future belongs to the few of us still willing to get our hands dirty." When I hear "roll up your sleeves" or "get your hands dirty," those analogies come from the thought that management wears long-sleeve, white collared shirts. Why, because we all work behind desks and don't get dirty, right? Not exactly. We have an office or desk and a computer because much of what we do is not necessarily on the front line. But hiding in an office can potentially give staff the impression that you don't care about them. I think rolling up the sleeve and going back out of the office and getting your hands dirty will be one of the best morale and culture builders you can do, if done consistently week in and week out. Go stand side by side with your team. As you work with them, ask them about their family, ask them about their weekend plans. But only if you truly care. Don't be fake. Don't just go through the motions because you read it in a book. Go be your genuine self. Watch what happens over time when you make this sort of commitment to joining the team and being one of them for a moment.

In my early days of management, I only had small teams of workers on shift at any given time and as a result, I was constantly working side by side with all of my people. This taught me the importance of learning about your colleagues' personal lives. I discovered some amazing things about my workers. Like some were guitar players in a band, others were lead actors in the local town theater, and others had kids and young families that I eventually got to meet. And they learned about me too. Met my wife, learned about the dogs I had, and what my hobbies were. We had an excellent connection that allowed me to better relate with them. There were also several times when I decided to do some duties that were not technically mine to do, but I didn't want any judgement from my employees about always delegating the less gratifying jobs to them.

I remember one time in my early days of managing, I was informed that a homeless gentleman had gone into one of our restrooms and essentially showered in the sink. I felt so bad that this poor guy desired to get clean and didn't have his own place to do it, but I certainly had some staff who were a bit disgusted by this act. If we go by job description alone, cleaning the restroom was certainly well below my pay grade. However, I didn't think twice. I grabbed some cleaner and a mop and headed to that bathroom.

In the heat of the moment, it all happened so fast, but that lone act would become what inspired the most loyal staff I ever worked with. They knew it was technically their job to do, but when they saw it wasn't below me, it changed some of their opinions. If by chance this exact scenario had happened again the following week, I could've asked any of them to clean the restroom and they wouldn't have even thought twice.

Setting the example. This is what they want to see to gain respect for their supervisor.

Speaking of asking them to do something, this is easily overlooked as a simple way to create a more cohesive, loyal team. There is a difference between asking your team to do something and telling them. If you implement many of the suggestions you're about to learn in this book, you will find you won't have to even ask—it will get done automatically by your team. My magic phrase, which I highly recommend you steal and use yourself, is "Can you do me a favor and . . .?" Human nature dictates that a person enjoys the act of doing another person a favor. I have asked for many favors in my leadership career, and it truly is a magical word.

Now my homeless bathroom story was just one example from an experience of mine. We are talking about setting a consistent example to let your employees know you are not this high and mighty person they have to fear. There is another reason we would want to set the example, though, and that would be to show them how something should be properly done. I understand that some companies have policies and procedures for training, but an employee tends to want to see something done properly so they can do it right. And who better to show them than their leader?

My wife used to be a store manager for Target, and here is what she shared Target does to ensure their employees are properly trained. "When managing for Target, I had the opportunity to train new leaders. Target had this concept down to four words: tell, show, do, review. You can start by telling but have to follow up with showing, doing, and reviewing (or practicing) to truly teach a new task."

Another great company that has mastered such systems is McDonald's.

McDonald's is an amazing organization that has had immense success over the decades it has been around. The consistency from restaurant to restaurant is fantastic. The food tends to taste the same no matter which location you go to, and the restrooms always seem to be clean and working properly. How does a company achieve this when they have over 36,000 locations in over one hundred countries? Three reasons: policies and procedures; immense training for the owners and leaders of each franchise; and leaders who lead by showing others in their stores how to do things right.

It would be easy to just pass instructions to an employee, but when things are demonstrated, especially by a leader, there won't be much room for failure.

I have spent sixteen years of my life in the military and as a result, I've been able to observe and learn what the military does and why. It always impresses me that when marching into harm's way, soldiers are typically led by their highest in command. In the true meaning of the word *leader*, the sergeant in a platoon leads with his men behind him. To me this is one of the truest forms of earning respect. You see, leadership must be earned, and I truly believe by doing the things you are asking others to do, leaders can take the quickest path to earning the respect of your staff and team. Another reason I like this soldier analogy is because in war, sometimes things get out of control and if that happens, people can die. The leader, the sergeant in my example, is responsible for keeping his or her troops calm in chaos. This is another way leaders can lead by example.

I remember during my days of running a real estate company, we would often have some of our agents call us in a panic because something went sideways with a home sale or a deal was getting ready to fall apart. They always seemed to be amazed that I didn't think the problems were as big as they seemed to be. Why, you may ask? Most of the time, I have been through the same thing, and so by sharing my experience with them, I show them that I too go through tough things, but I've got solutions for them as their leader.

Many years ago, I had a job as a courtesy clerk. If you have ever worked in the supermarket industry or been part of the food workers union, you likely know what a courtesy clerk is. It is the person who bags groceries at your local store. Well, in 1990 I was growing up in a small town in the mountains of Southern California called Big Bear Lake. I desired a new job and applied at a Vons grocery store up there. It was where my mom shopped, so it made sense. I applied and the store manager, Russ, hired me and I was off and running. Courtesy clerk is really an entry-level job at a grocery store, and it's typically where all new employees start, then earn their way up to maybe a checker, department manager, assistant manager, and then eventually to Russ's job, store manager. So imagine my surprise when I saw Russ bagging groceries every day. Not for his entire shift, not even for more than a customer or two. But it was practically every day I saw him. Why? Well, because we got busy, and we never have enough courtesy clerks working as checkers. I don't think Russ knew that he was earning my respect by doing it, but he absolutely was. The job wasn't below him. Neither was grabbing the heavy bags of dog food that I was often asked to load into customer's shopping carts. Russ certainly could've barked orders for us courtesy clerks to work faster or demand the checkers bag their own groceries, which they certainly did at times. Ultimately, it was a customer service element that led to earned respect from all who saw him do this. It wasn't just bagging groceries. I saw Russ stock products on shelves, slice meat in the deli, tie off a bale of cardboard for recycling, and so much more. Russ was a busy guy, and I respected the heck out of him. As a result, I worked very hard for Russ. If he ever asked me to do a job that wasn't technically in my job description, I would do it, because I saw him do it daily.

If you are a leader, it's important to reflect on your duties and the duties of those below you. Do you think you've led by example? Can you think of specific times in which you did? What about your own personal growth and development? Later in the book I have a chapter on this topic, but this is a great time to introduce it since several of my research respondents mentioned personal development as an area they'd like to see their supervisors leading by example in. In fact, Samantha Alley from Corvallis, Oregon, said, "If you want your team to grow and get better, how can you lead them if *you* don't? I am more willing to follow someone who shows an interest in getting better." This was a fantastic perspective since so many of my respondents used the phrase "lead from the front."

There also seems to be a muted sense of caring the higher up the chain you go. Michelle Caietta from South Carolina says, "When I had a bigger issue that was escalated, the higher up it went, the less people seemed to care. I think leadership cares less when the immediate person is not there right in front of them, when those leaders aren't the ones looking someone in the eyes and denying their request or addressing the issue."

Michelle brings up a great point in that if we find ourselves several rungs up the leadership ladder, we must not forget to occasionally go down a few rungs and build rapport with the lower-level teams so that we know the people in which our decisions affect.

Whether you are an upper C-level executive, or a lower-level department manager, we must consistently find ways to lead from the front. It's the sole reason why the TV show *Undercover Boss* has become so popular over the years. CEOs and other leaders at companies are finding so much value in working undercover, side by side with their workers. They gain so much intel in doing so. Talking with the folks who show you what's broken and maybe why some of your business objectives aren't being met. If we stay cooped up in an office all the time, we rely on suspicion and assumptions. Instead, get out there, and talk with your people. Just like on *Undercover Boss*, you will discover who your workforce is and the real-life personal struggles they sometimes endure.

And when you are at the front, all eyes are on you. They will watch what you do. The good habits and the bad ones. That's right. Even the bad habits they will see. It is very important that we don't do the things we don't want our staff to do.

> The reality is that the only way change comes is when you lead by example.
>
> —Anne Wojcicki, CEO of 23andMe

Action Steps for "Leading by Example"

1. Reflect on your duties as a leader and the duties of those below you. Have you done some of the duties of your workers? If so, which ones?

    _____

    _____

    _____

    _____

    _____

If not, what duties do you feel could be good for leading by example?

_____

_____

_____

2. If you have leaders below you who also lead a team, have you witnessed them leading by example? If so, how?

_____

_____

_____

Now take time to acknowledge their leadership if they have led by example. If they have not, maybe share a copy of this book with them, or give them ideas on how they can earn their team's trust by leading by example and showing their team that those tasks aren't below them.

3. Think about what habits you have that may be hurting you as a leader. Are you leading by example in a bad way? If so, how can you change those habits so that your team doesn't judge you for them? (Showing up late, taking tons of unnecessary smoke breaks, etc.)

_____

_____

_____

_____

_____

4. Think of someone on your team who is struggling with a task. Can you apply tell, show, do, review to get them comfortable? If so, who on your team should experience this level of leadership care?

_____

_____

_____

_____

_____

CHAPTER 2

Don't Manage
the Micro Way

> In most cases being a good boss means hiring talented people and then getting out of their way.
>
> —Tina Fey, comedian

Have you ever felt like a manager was breathing down your neck? Or maybe you have had managers hover over you to make sure you did your job exactly the way they expect. Bosses do have a job to do, and one of those things is to ensure all workers are doing the things they are supposed to be doing. However, what gets missed is the method by which you accomplish these checks and balances.

Most of us do not want to be checked on. We want to feel like we've earned the trust of our employers and that they are empowering us to do the job right. You see, it's not good when you don't feel trusted by your boss. Your sense of accomplishment goes away, and your job satisfaction is definitely affected. Eventually you likely will quit that job. This turnover, which many companies experience, often comes as a result of micromanaging.

Merriam-Webster defines micromanaging as a verb meaning "to manage especially with excessive control." Do you like your boss to be excessive in nature as it pertains to your job? Do you want to feel controlled? Probably not, and this is why micromanaging came up as something most employees do not like seeing in their workplace.

It does boil down to trust. A manager assigns tasks, maybe even with a deadline. But they are nervous whether it will get done right and on time, so they constantly check in and hover to ensure it does get done. This doesn't sound too terribly bad as a concept, but the employee is the one who suffers here. The lack of trust that they can do the job right and complete it on time causes animosity between boss and worker.

There is a better way to achieve the same result.

Have you ever used a training calendar? A training calendar maps out different aspects of one's job, which we will focus on for training. It also says what day they will learn a specific duty and who will be training them. The training calendar allows a new employee to get fully trained to ensure nothing gets missed. Investing time in the front end will ensure the job gets done exactly the way you want, without having to micromanage. If they do mess something up, then you need to look in the mirror. In *Are You a Manager or a Leader?*, I have an entire chapter called "Looking in the Mirror." The idea behind this is to reflect and see if you, as the manager, were possibly at fault in any given situation or if the error could have been prevented. Maybe you forgot to provide training on an important aspect of the worker's job. Maybe you didn't stress the importance of timelines and deadlines. Looking in the mirror allows us to show the employee:

1. We will train you properly and thoroughly; and
2. We won't assume you were at fault should you make an error.

Now this doesn't mean that the employee isn't at fault; it just means we are empowering the employee to make the right decisions based on their training, and should something go wrong, we will look to ourselves first before any corrective action or retraining. In these circumstances we have to be patient. We will be talking quite a bit more about patience later in the book.

Another great exhibit of leading by example came from one of my survey respondents who works in a restaurant as a server. "I walked into work the other day, and my boss was scrubbing the stairs! Even though it was on the list of 'maintenance projects' that people can sign up to do for extra time on the clock, he had time and decided to help. It showed me he really cares about the place, and he's not above anyone else in the sense that he's willing to get dirty and use some elbow grease now and then. Since then, I've seen more people do a little more each day. My goal is to always go above and beyond in some area each day." I really am impressed with how, after witnessing this act from her manager, she wanted to do more and work harder at her job. It was a great surprise to see this positive attitude come from this small act.

I share these personal stories from everyday individuals because, as leaders, we truly have to understand how to best lead, and one way to accomplish this is by getting the perspective of our people. In *Are You a Manager or a Leader?*, I talk about my experience turning two different high-volume retail locations from losing money for several years to making a profit in just four short months. I was hired as a general manager and brought in to specific locations because of my track record with the company of increasing profit and reducing turnover. How? I analyzed the profit and loss statements and realized how much we were spending on training and hiring. For a company these can be huge expense lines, and for me it was. So I decided to create a strategic plan to reduce turnover. It started with me getting the perception and advice of the people in my employ. What do they want to see more of? How do they like to be managed? Paying attention to your staff and asking lots of questions will not only reduce turnover and increase profits, but employees become more loyal and happier.

I understand there are circumstances in which a boss may not be able to actually work side by side with you or do work for you. In my efforts to get real thoughts on this topic, I had one person mention that he works in a union and so his boss truly is not able to do any of his work per union contract. He did go on to say this, though, which I think is relevant for any leader who maybe is in this scenario: "My supervisor listened and really considered our opinions and communicated clearly. He asked a lot out of us, but he asked in a way that empowered and challenged us to achieve what he was asking."

Empower—the definition is to give power, rights, or authority to do something. Most of the workers in a workforce like the feeling of leaders empowering them to make good decisions. I used to say to my staff, "I trust you to do a great job. If for some reason something doesn't come out the way I was expecting, then we will have a quick conversation about it and move on. But I'd rather you have the power to get this done with minimal input by me and just come to me if you get stuck or need more guidance." This is empowering. Give them the power, and if something goes wrong, we can always correct it. Your staff will tend to stay with your company longer and will be happier in their job. BusinessNewsDaily.com published an article called "12 Secrets to Keeping Employees Happy Without a Raise" and number eight was to empower them. In that article, Zachary Watson, associate at Greenberg Gross LLP, has a great quote about it: "If you're looking to keep an employee by giving [them] a raise, it's already too late. Find people who share the operational values of your organization from the outset, test for fit early and allow growth opportunities to express that value."

One response I received gave great detail about how a micromanager completely changed the amazing attitude of one of the company's top employees, which ultimately led her to leave the company. She stated, "I was thrilled to have earned a big promotion. Little did I know that promotion made my direct supervisor a micromanager. It was her way and her way only. If there was a project, there was never a time where a target was delivered without exact instructions of how she expected the target to be met, no exceptions, no other opinions, no other way. To make it worse, on the rare occasion her supervisor came to check in, if they asked about something being different than company expectation, she instantly threw whoever was there under the bus. I went from excited about a promotion to leaving the company all together two years later."

It's sad when I hear stories like this because they are 100 percent avoidable. This happens as a result of a higher-up having control issues. As you climb the ladder at work, know that there are people on those lower rungs doing work they know how to do already. They don't need us dictating their every move. Delegating is one of the perks in growing with a company. We have to learn to let go of control on those tasks, though. This is what it means to empower. To me it almost means trust. Give someone a task to do, and trust it will get done properly. Likely it will if your staff was trained properly. As soon as we interfere with how the task should be done and check in several times asking if they are working on it, they start to get frustrated and wonder if we even trust them. No one wants to feel like they aren't worthy of doing a simple task. Should the task be done by a certain deadline? Maybe. If so, give them that deadline. But if they've never shown you that they can't meet deadlines properly, leave them alone. Empower them to take on the task. They will appreciate the trust, do the task well, and stay with you for years.

This is not to say that we still don't want to properly train our people. Just hiring and advocating for the job rarely works and typically leads to a frustrated employee who quits. We still need to show them what their job is and how to do it. Then give them the projects you want and empower them to do things with minimal supervision.

Signs of a micromanager include overcommunication, not delegating enough, and not giving others room to make decisions on how to achieve the desired result. If you fear you may be micromanaging, consider what the worst-case scenario would be if you did not micromanage the next project. What is the best-case scenario? For the next project you assign to a report, let them know the desired outcome and that you know they have the ability to figure out how best to achieve it. Take a deep breath, step back, and see what happens.

Jody Scott from Edmonds, Washington, shared, "My boss would often come by my office and ask me how my caseload was and if he could help." This is a great demonstration of care and leading from the front. Checking in and just asking, "How are things going? Anything you need from me?" can go a long way.

In my efforts to discover why micromanaging is such a detriment to a company, one leader at a Fortune 500 company said, "I think micromanagers stifle one's creativity, where someone who empowers, listens to others, includes their ideas, or adopts them outright. Those who are described as empowering tend to be great listeners. That's important because everyone wants to be heard!"

The word *empower* came up frequently in my quest to discover the key traits that workers seek in their leader. In fact, I'll end this chapter with a great quote from Nasdaq CEO Adena Friedman, who says, "Empowering those around you to be heard and valued makes the difference between a leader who simply instructs and one who inspires."

Action Steps for "Don't Manage the Micro Way"

1. After reading this chapter, do you feel you are a micromanager? YES NO (circle one)

2. If YES, what can you do differently to change this habit and start showing your team that you trust them more?

_____

_____

_____

_____

3. Have you ever received complaints because you micromanage, or has your turnover been high (which can also be from micromanaging your team)? YES NO (circle one)

4. How can you ensure that the leaders below you who also are managing a team aren't micromanaging?

_____

_____

_____

_____

CHAPTER 3

Do You Even Care?
Are You Impatient?

> Nobody cares how much you know until they know how much you care.
>
> —Theodore Roosevelt

"Caring is leadership," offered one of my respondents, Jonathon Lerche from Ithaca, New York. This is a powerful yet short statement. Egos can be dangerous. And when it comes to bosses or supervisors, many times we want to make sure our team knows why we got to where we are today. Often, we believe they should respect us just because we are their boss and our title at our company says they should respect us. But, as you learned in the last chapter, respect is not given— it is earned. And it needs to be earned by every employee and re-earned often. I like the quote that starts out this chapter because it is a constant reminder to keep your ego in check. Don't brag about how much you know or how good you are.

Your team doesn't care about that. Unless they already know how much you care about them. I learned years ago that my team is not a team because of me. It's a team because of them, and we are only as strong as our weakest person. It is up to me to identify all of this, lift my people up, and arm them with the proper tools and resources so that they can be successful within their respective jobs.

In my other book on leadership, I have an entire chapter on the subject of caring. Chapter 11 in that book is titled "Leaders Reflect and Show Care." In the chapter, one of the key ways in which to help demonstrate care is writing your team personal, handwritten notes. At the peak of my leadership, I would write five notes per week to my people. Not an email—a personal card. Email is too formal and businesslike. A handwritten note takes time to actually write. And I'm not talking about using those companies that have software that will make it look like you wrote the note. No! I'm talking old school, get out a pen and make it happen. Because it takes time, it will be very well received by the recipient. Think about this . . . When you receive a personal, handwritten note from someone, how does it make you feel? For me, fantastic! That someone took the time to write to me when rarely anyone does anymore—incredible. In fact, I personally save every note that gets sent to me. I cherish them and when I'm having a bad day, I go through them, and it instantly cheers me up. I recently went through these old notes and found some from seventeen years ago. Some brought tears to my eyes. You never know when someone is in need of a touching note card of care. You want to put a smile on an employee's face? Want to gain more loyalty? Want to inspire your team? Write notes.

Make note writing part of your daily habit. Try not to be selective either. We use an Excel document to make sure we are writing notes to all of our people throughout the year. Yes, some may get more over the course of the year, but we try to make sure that everyone gets a note. As a professional coach today, I come across many individuals who struggle with writing notes. You might wonder what to say in the note. Here are a few suggestions to get you thinking about what to say:

- "How are you and your family doing?" (This shows care not just for them but also their family life.)

- "Great job on that project or task." (This shows them that you pay attention and they impressed you.)

- "Great chatting with you earlier today." (This would be great if you ran into them in the hallway, breakroom, parking lot, etc.)

- "If you ever need help with anything, please reach out to me." (This shows transparency and that you have an open door.)

The biggest key in this is to not overthink it. The more you do, the easier it becomes. And don't stop just at staff. Think about vendors, the mail person, UPS and FedEx drivers, and neighboring businesses. I have found that over time, all of these personal notes of care come back to you. I mean literally. You will start to see some of these folks sending you personal notes. That's how you know you made an impact. Now you're back to leading by example, and in this case, the example is note writing.

One of the biggest ways you'll know that these notes of care are well received is when you visit that employee's work area. You'll start to see that note you wrote them months ago pinned on the wall or taped near their computer at their desk. That's why I keep writing notes. They need words of encouragement, and whom else to receive them from but their leader?

I do believe that this is a great place for me to add a note on journaling. Great leaders reflect on their day and many journal. I want to encourage you to start a habit (if you don't already have one) of writing in a journal each day. Again, you may ask, "But what do I journal about?" Start with the positives of the day. The good stuff. Often, we get home from work and are exhausted, burnt out, and feeling like we didn't get anything done. But the truth is, you did. And you likely had staff who did great things today. Journal about that. Almost view it like a gratitude journal. You'll start to find the good in people by doing this versus focusing on what they are doing wrong. This will help swing the pendulum toward better loyalty from your people.

When I hit the streets and asked what are some ways that a supervisor or leader can show care, one of the most impactful ways mentioned was by listening. "They care by listening and actually hearing what you say, even if they don't agree with it. They care by paying attention to you and your work," says one respondent regarding the topic. Another respondent stated, "They want to be heard and understood. I think that's one of the best ways to show you care no matter if it's in their personal life or business life."

In my research, listening and understanding came up a ton as what employees seek from their supervisors. They want to feel part of something larger than themselves. They want to feel like they've contributed to the company or the project. A bank manager friend of mine put it this way: "Asking and expecting feedback around company decisions is crucial to the team feeling valued and to the company in keeping their fingers on the pulse of their clients and what's happening with their clients and teams." Oftentimes as leaders, we don't have the luxury of being on the front line; our people are closer to customers than we are. So asking them for their advice and then listening can be huge for business, and it certainly shows the employee that you value their thoughts and opinions.

Listening is definitely a key leadership trait. If you have heard me speak before, you may have heard the story about how in meetings I used to rarely listen to others' opinions. It was my way or the highway, and no one was going to have better ideas than me, right? Wrong. In fact, John C. Maxwell says in his book *Developing the Leaders Around You* that "every idea is a good idea until you've settled on the best idea." I learned the hard way that listening and understanding takes you so much farther. I had found that many times I had good ideas for our company, but my team had better ones. If you can create a culture around consistently asking questions from your team and soliciting feedback from them on various topics, they will quickly understand how much you care about them and their jobs. In fact, I had several individuals share that they sometimes don't even need anything necessarily fixed as much as they sometimes just want to say things out loud to feel better.

I absolutely love this comment about how to show care from one of my respondents: "It doesn't matter what role or title you hold, showing people that you care is vital to both your soul and the soul of the receiver. After all, we work to live, not live to work, right? Therefore, we should value humans before work. Which means we hire to a vision and ask who do they see themselves becoming in this process? That shows you care about them as much as where you are going."

Earlier I mentioned the importance and impact of writing personal notes of care to your people. Well, another way that you can show care is by sending video messages to your people on occasion. In my other leadership book, I have an entire chapter on leading through video, and I tell many stories that demonstrate ways to do this, not just with your own employees but also on social media and in front of consumers.

I use a platform called BombBomb to send my videos, and I've sent thousands over the years. (I know this only because BombBomb tracks how many you've sent.) What I love about BombBomb is it easily allows you to record a short video, re-record if necessary, and send to your employee(s). Similar to the ideas behind writing a personal note, I would use video to show emotion on my face to my people. You see, using only words doesn't always get the point across. But imagine you saw an employee go out of their way for a customer. You can certainly go see them face-to-face and say, "great job!" and I sometimes do that, for sure. But I have also sent this message many times through video message. They see the emotion on your face, they hear the inflection in your voice, and they can tell you truly care. That video is something they can rewatch when they are having an off day. I've had employees tell me that they do this, and it encourages me to catch them doing great things again and send more. They also say things like, "Thanks for sending me that video. I showed it to my wife because it truly made my day, and then it put a smile also on my wife's face." Unintentionally, I am now reaching my employee's home life with care. The family now sees that I care about my people.

Enough to stop my busy day and send a video. Also, if you happen to use software like BombBomb, they have a feature where the recipient can actually reply immediately to your video. Another cool way to stay connected with your people.

Speaking of showing care through video, one of the best things you can do is send a happy birthday video to your staff. Often in today's busy world, the best we do is comment on someone's Facebook page wishing them a happy birthday. We need to get better, and we need to be different. I think a Facebook post or comment is the minimum expectation. But we want to go above and beyond to truly show care. I had a mentor of mine, Brian Buffini, who always said, "We must have some *unexpected extras* in order to more quickly grow trust and a relationship."

Sending a video, a gift, or even a personalized card on their birthday is always going to stand out compared to what that employee was likely used to from past employers. And when we stand out, they recruit other great employees to us, making our hiring easier. I cannot tell you how many times I've sung "Happy Birthday" to a staff member. They get to see the goofy side of me too, which humanizes me. I am no longer Scott the Scary Boss. I am a caring leader who not only remembered their birthday but also stopped for a moment in my day to do this. Do you have a spouse who plays piano or guitar? My wife plays the piano—well, she's trying to learn—but she learned "Happy Birthday." Get someone to play an instrument while you sing "Happy Birthday," and it adds another element of care because now someone else is involved in the birthday wishes.

You'll also find that everyone wants to be managed differently. One of the best ways to demonstrate care is opening yourself up to managing and leading your people the way they prefer to be led. Let me give you an example: I must give some feedback to a staff person about a task they are doing for me. Are they the type of person who prefers face-to-face feedback, or does that intimidate them? Would they prefer an email outlining the feedback so that it's in writing for them and can be referenced again later? Do they want you to stop them right away and give them direct feedback each time you notice something that needs to be corrected, or would they prefer, maybe at the end of each day or week, bullet pointing all of the things that need to be done differently? I could go on, but you get the point. Everyone is different, and even asking them what their preferred method of feedback delivery is shows care. Simon Sinek says, "Leadership is not about being in charge, it's about taking care of those in your charge."

And then of course there's being patient with our people. Patience came up frequently in our initial survey about what makes a great leader. Why? You can look to bad managers and supervisors to get this answer. I believe those managers who pass a snap judgement or jump to conclusions are going to have much higher staff turnover and ultimately, they won't be successful in their roles. We must be patient as leaders. Another one of my survey responders, Bob Koch from South Carolina, says, "I have to remind myself that I have to show my employees patience and assist them with their tasks early in their career." Bob understands that this investment of his time as a leader and his money (payroll dollars) will pay dividends later in that employee's career. It takes time to properly develop someone, but it is up to us, and we must be patient as they grow into the role.

Kari Zimmerman from Snohomish, Washington, agreed on the importance of a leader having patience, stating, "A leader with a lack of patience can result in a team who is afraid to ask questions, afraid to take risks or make tough decisions, and reluctant to take initiative. This stunts the growth of both the team members and the organization as a whole. It's a disservice to everyone." As leaders, we may understand what patience is, and maybe even understand that it should play a role in our management of people; however, the examples we kept getting on the topic truly made me feel like it needs to be higher on our radar than we thought. I had yet another respondent say, "Patience is crucial because impatience can breed a lack of trust. Example: If I look to a leader for guidance and he/she is impatient with me, I feel like I am an annoyance or a burden, and I naturally want to withdraw and will hesitate to go to that person again and ultimately avoid going to that person after repeat instances of displayed impatience. I will not feel 'safe' going to them." Thank you, Gia Commodore, for this great example. The last thing we would want as leaders is to break trust and become unapproachable.

Caring for an employee's growth in their role is huge for so many workers. Investing time with those individuals to make sure they have the best chance at moving up in the company can make an employee loyal to you and the company. Showing a level of care outside the workforce can be even more impactful at times. Things like working with an employee's shift times to accommodate their personal life. Regarding why people left a company, we saw on the survey I conducted that "better hours" was top six on that list. My wife actually had an experience at one of her former jobs where her immediate supervisor even went as far as to offer suggestions on the company's stock purchase plan and 401k. Here's what my wife, Renee, said regarding that experience: "When I was a new leader at

Target, Ed Z. was my store manager. He provided guidance for my overall future, such as recommending contributing to my retirement account. As a twenty-one-year-old, it wasn't something I was familiar with. He took the time to explain a high-level overview of investing and compounding interest and even made a suggestion to start with a certain amount and to increase my contribution each time I received a raise. This has been life-changing advice!" What's very interesting about this is that my wife and I have become very passionate about helping others achieve financial freedom for many years, and I see now where one of those influences came from. So I guess you can see that simple conversations that show care can even reach the spouse and family of your workers. Never underestimate the impact you might have by showing a little bit of care.

As you can see, there are many ways to show care at your workplace, and my goal is to give you some of the best of what research has shown and what I've personally seen work. One last idea I will leave you with is giving small gifts of appreciation on occasion. I owned a large real estate brokerage in the Seattle area, and as we grew, it became more and more challenging to show care and remember the little things that matter to your people. As a result, we decided to use what we called a favorites form. On it, we asked our people what their favorite things were. Favorite candy bar (in case we decided to get them a little snack and leave it on their desk), favorite restaurant (for when they had a birthday so we could possibly get them their favorite meal), favorite type of music, favorite sports team, and so on. I cannot tell you how many times we referenced these favorites forms to get our people something they like when we wanted to reward them. In fact, often they would end up posting pictures of the candy bar, gift card, or other gift, mentioning how they work at the best company. These were such small gestures and small gifts, but the impact it made, and the way the employees felt, helped them become just a bit more dedicated and loyal to us.

We started this chapter with a quote, and I want to end with another, from Maya Angelou. "People will forget what you said, people will forget what you did, but people will never forget how you made them feel."

Action Steps for "Do You Even Care?"

1. Do you feel like you currently show care? YES NO (circle one)

   Take a few moments to reflect on what you've done in the past to show care and ask yourself if it's enough. Use this space to record your thoughts.

   _____

   _____

   _____

   _____

   _____

   _____

   _____

   _____

   _____

2. Think of five individuals in your environment to write a personal note to and demonstrate that you care about the work they do for you and your company. Write those names here.

a. _____

b. _____

c. _____

d. _____

e. _____

3. Active Listening: Do you feel like you have conversations with your people where they get a voice and you truly listen to their ideas and/or complaints? Use this space to jot down ways to get better at listening.

_____

_____

_____

_____

4. Explore the idea of incorporating video messaging into your weekly routines with your staff. Maybe check out video messaging platforms like BombBomb. What can this look like for you?

_____

_____

_____

_____

5. How's your patience with the people within your employ? Does it need some work? Journal here about how you feel regarding this topic.

_____

_____

_____

_____

CHAPTER 4

How's Your Communication?

> Leadership is a way of thinking, a way of acting and, most importantly, a way of communicating.
>
> —Simon Sinek, bestselling author and motivational speaker

How is your communication? Can it be improved? Well, it didn't surprise me, when I surveyed several individuals on the topic of leadership, that great communication was one of the top responses as a trait a leader needs. There is a quote I heard years ago that will always resonate with me: "Conflict only arises when expectations differ." Your team won't make mistakes if their tasks are clearly communicated. A deadline won't get missed if it is clearly communicated. And if something goes wrong, we must reflect and ask ourselves how we could avoid this scenario in the future. In *Are You a Manager or a Leader?*, I have an entire chapter called "Look in the Mirror."

In this chapter I share how good leaders always reflect on how something went wrong before jumping to conclusions and disciplining their people. Oftentimes it comes back to the way we originally communicated or maybe the lack of that communication.

Also, if you have other managers in your organization below you, they too must embrace the concept of looking in the mirror.

In McDonald's franchisee training for owner/operators, they have an entire segment on how to improve your active listening skills. Here is a simplified version of what they share:

1. Active listening—demonstrate through your actions (eye contact, nodding your head, and affirmative noises).

2. Don't interrupt—let the employees finish their thought before you reply. Avoid guessing where their thoughts are going.

3. Ask questions—one way to show you are listening is to ask questions about what's being said.

4. Repeat back—repeat back what was said but in your own words. If by chance you misunderstood them, then this gives them a chance to correct.

5. Total meaning—any message contains what is being said but also the attitude behind it. Sometimes the real message is in the emotion or attitude, so pay attention.

As we shared in the prior chapter on care, active listening and asking questions are extremely important to a successful working relationship. Not just because it shows care, but it is also crucial to the success of the task and job at hand. A company can grow quicker if it instills these key things into their teams. I know it's worked for McDonalds and many other companies alike.

There are several podcasts out there that can help with improving your communication. If you search your favorite place to listen to podcasts (Google, Apple, Spotify, etc.), you will find some options for learning to better your communication.

Brian Tracy is my absolute favorite author, and he has a quote that reads as follows: "Communication is a skill that you can learn. It's like riding a bicycle or typing. If you're willing to work at it, you can rapidly improve the quality of every part of your life." Speaking of authors and books, there have been several great books on the topic, and I always encourage folks to find one that resonates with them. Some of the highest-rated communication books on Amazon are:

- *7L: The Seven Levels of Communication* by Michael J. Maher
- *How to Talk to Anybody* by Derek Borthwick
- *Effective Communication Skills* by Saif Hussaini
- *Communication Skills Training* by Ian Tuhovsky
- *Listen Well, Lead Better* by Steve Harling and Becky Harling

I've also read a book that I highly recommend to anyone who owns a business, wants to start a business, or is a leader—*Who Not How* by Dan Sullivan. This book helps you realize that you don't need to know how to do everything to be successful at something, as long as you either know or can find the who. In other words, if you aren't great at communication, search for the person who is and learn from them. That's why I always recommend searching for a great book or podcast to improve those weaker skills.

In my days of owning a real estate brokerage, we always recommended to our salespeople that they take courses and earn designations. One of the top designations we recommended was the RENE (Real Estate Negotiation Expert) certification. One of the things taught in this negotiation course is that to get better at negotiation, we must communicate with the other party ideally the way they prefer to be communicated with. In other words, some realtors prefer text communication, some prefer calls. Yet others just want an email, and some actually prefer in person. If you find yourself communicating this way with your competitor, your clients, and vendors alike, you will find success more frequently, as you are instantly eliminating a roadblock toward winning them over.

Another way put, if your employees prefer face-to-face communication, then make the time to deliver messages that way. If they prefer a simple text, done. You will find they like it better and will respect you more as a leader by asking their preferred communication style. I do need to say that for difficult conversations or constructive feedback, use the method best for that scenario. In this case, I would refer to the communication pyramid illustrated in the bestselling book, *7L: The Seven Levels of Communication.* Just an FYI, this book was written mostly for the sales community as a way to help salespeople close more deals and get more referrals. But I have found that the foundational concept of the book and this pyramid work in many facets of life and business.

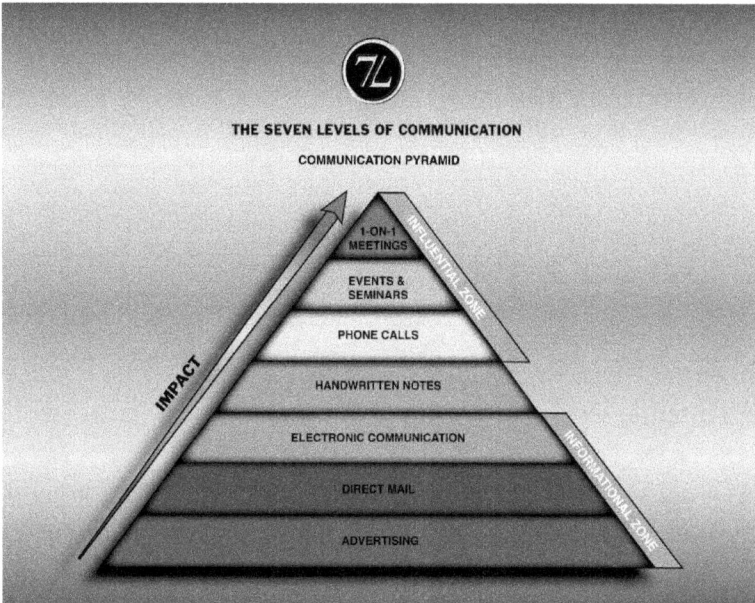

The tougher the communication, the higher on the pyramid you need to go for delivery of the message. This is missing text messages and video, both of which I would put in the Influential Zone toward the top of the pyramid. The one-on-one meeting is the most effective for influencing people, so bear this in mind when considering how to communicate messages.

Video can be an amazing way of communicating with your people, as mentioned earlier in this book. We discussed the benefits of using it as a retention tool to deliver messages that show care. But don't forget that video can be a great tool for simple communication as well. Especially if you use an app like we discussed earlier, where you can send or screen share videos to others. You can demonstrate something to your staff, simply through video. Or give an update on a project, simply through video. Just remember the rule we shared earlier: if the message would be better sent as a video versus a regular email, then send the video.

> The most important thing in communication is to hear what isn't being said.
>
> —Peter F. Drucker, Austrian-American consultant and educator

As we have conversations with others in our organization, both upper-level folks and our direct employees, there are often key things that aren't said. When conversing with our teams, we must listen and look for silent cues. This can especially come into play around the topic of empathy and trying to understand why someone may be acting or performing in a certain way. Occasionally your people won't tell you what the problem is, but if you watch for facial expressions or overall demeanor, this may tip you off that something is not being said, and this would be a good time to then ask the question, "Is there anything further you'd like to share?"

Action Steps for "How's Your Communication?"

1. On a scale of 1 to 10 (1 being weak and 10 being amazing), how would you rate your own communication and why?

    _____

    _____

    _____

2. If you need help with your communication skills as a leader, what steps can you take within the next thirty days to start improving?

_____

_____

_____

_____

3. How do you like to be communicated with most? Text message, call, email, or in person?

_____

_____

4. How do your staff, salespeople, and vendors prefer to be communicated with? (If you don't know, can you ask and find out?)

_____

_____

_____

_____

CHAPTER 5

Have a Personal Development Plan

> I cannot remember the books I've read any more than the meals I have eaten; even so, they have made me.
>
> —Ralph Waldo Emerson, American essayist

Probably one of my top five quotes is that one from Ralph Waldo Emerson, because it is a constant reminder of the power of personal development. He knew that by reading books, he would garner the experience and knowledge of the author. It's one of the things I love about books.

Ralph Waldo Emerson was born in 1803 and really, books were all they had for personal growth. And back then, not everyone knew how to read or had access to books. Over the years, people have been able to tap into more and more ways of improving themselves, from records to audiotapes to attending conferences. In recent times, we have found the more impactful way of self-improvement is through reading (or audiobooks) and also podcasts. Most books that have been written on a self-improvement topic have been a 150–200-page summary of the author's twenty to thirty years of experience on that topic. That is incredible, right? The fact that we get to fast-track our way to learning from someone who made mistakes (so we don't make the same mistakes) and had successes (so we don't have to figure those out for ourselves) is magical. Now imagine reading a book a month for a year. If you were careful at selecting topics that you need improvement on, you will more quickly get to your goals and level of success. The way I see it is that a book a month (ten pages a day of reading) can get me to over 240 years of combined experience over the course of a calendar year from some of the best and most successful individuals on topics I need to get better at. Now let me motivate you even more. Do you have a competitor? Maybe another employee seeking the same promotion as you? Or maybe it's another business you compete against. Imagine that they don't read a book a month for the next year, but you do. All of the knowledge you gain during that year will create a compound effect in your life and business. This is how you win.

With podcasts, what I love most about them are two things: First, they don't cost you anything. It used to be back in Ralph Waldo Emerson's days that you would need to pay for this wisdom, and more recently motivational guys like Zig Ziglar would sell you their tape or CD series on being a better leader or whatever topic they had back then. With podcasts, you have experts on different topics sharing their best stuff at no cost. It has been one of the best ways I've personally plugged into growing my knowledge. Second, podcasts give you the ability to fill up empty time, like commuting. Play a helpful podcast on your way to work or an appointment instead of listening to the morning show on your radio. Day after day, week after week, year after year of this, and you will be transformed.

But is it important for a leader to have a personal development plan? And do their employees even care if they do? After all, how does a personal development plan for a leader even benefit the people under them? Well, we posed this question in our research, and the response was pretty unanimous that yes, employees want a leader who focuses on continued growth for themselves. Why? Many reasons were shared by my respondents, and I will share some of those now to give you insight. My former business coach, Tyrone Davids from Toronto, says this: "The real reason why they should be looking to constantly improve is that it creates a posture of learning. This humble posture enables them to listen, collaborate, and realize they can never have all of the answers. That attitude is present in all great leaders."

A friend of mine, Maureen Butwin from South Carolina, says this, "I feel it is very important for the leader/manager to continue to grow and learn how things can always be done better so that they can pass that knowledge and training on to their employees. Knowledge is key and power! The more you know, the stronger you will be and your business will be!"

This statement reminds me of the old NBC snippets during commercial breaks where they would share a quick fact about something, and then they would put these words on the screen: The More You Know! Knowledge truly is power, but in order to gain the right knowledge, we must have an actual plan to achieve the right development results.

Jim Rohn is one of the top business minds to ever train and speak on stage, and he says, "An investment in your personal development is the best investment you can make." So we have to invest the time and money necessary to allow this to transpire for us. But how much money should we invest? Well, Brian Tracy has stated for years that his strong recommendation is 3 percent of your income back into yourself. If you make $100,000 a year, then that would be $3,000 per year on growth. If you make $200,000 a year, then double that to $6,000 that you should invest into yourself. You might ask, "Is this absolutely necessary?" I would argue that it's crucial.

This means budget for it. Don't end the year with anything left in that personal development bucket. If there is toward the end of the year, then take an impromptu trip to an industry conference, leadership conference, or buy some courses or books to help you accelerate your knowledge and growth.

My wife and I have followed this plan for years and trained others to do the same, and the dividends are compounded year over year, and your whole life starts to be affected positively. In fact, *New York Times* bestselling author Darren Hardy talks about this investment in yourself in his book *The Compound Effect*. In this book, Darren mentions how anyone can achieve amazing massive growth. Just not overnight. Little by little, improve yourself to be better today than yesterday. If you are intrigued by this and possibly want to start implementing this sort of investment into yourself but don't know what a personal growth plan can look like, maybe watch Brian Tracy's YouTube video titled "5 Ways to Invest in Yourself." In this Brian covers:

- importance of continuous learning
- improving your skills
- setting aside personal time
- exploring creative outlets

- prioritizing personal health
- measuring personal growth

It's just a fourteen-minute video and can get you headed in the right direction with a good game plan to grow.

I also had several individuals mention "leading from the front." This goes back to chapter 1, "Be One of Them." It is extremely important that our team continues to adapt with the times by introducing new technology into the workplace and finding better ways of doing things that are more effective and efficient. The only way for our team to do this is if we do. We must have a plan to be successful leaders and create a plan for our people.

As my former colleague Charlie Foxworth from Austin, Texas, says, "If you want those that follow you to be consistent and grow, you must be willing to do the same."

The moral of this story is that improving in your weaknesses is better for your bottom line. Humble yourself and find out what those areas are for you. Seek to improve yourself. Many leaders invest in a business coach, and I am no exception. I would not be where I am today without the help and accountability of each of my coaches.

For years I have taught the concept of doing a personal development self-audit. It is something that I eventually incorporated into the business planning session I host at the end of each year. It essentially asks a series of questions to reflect on the prior twelve months so that you can create a solid plan for the next twelve months. Some of those questions I've posed in our action steps for this chapter.

Action Steps for "Have a Personal Development Plan"

1. What skill(s) do you need to improve? (Employee communication, hiring, coaching, negotiating, etc.)

_____

_____

_____

_____

2. Pick a book to read on a topic that you need to improve on. There is a recommended book list in the back of this book for reference. Write the name of the book you will read here with the date that you plan to finish reading it by.

_____

_____

_____

_____

3. Select a new podcast to listen to and then listen to an episode on a subject that you would like to elevate your game in. What podcast did you select?

_____

_____

_____

_____

4. What consistent plan will you immediately put in place for yourself that will help you move the needle on personal growth?

_____

_____

_____

_____

_____

5. Watch the YouTube video from Brian Tracy titled "5 Ways to Invest in Yourself." Then reflect on what you learned below.

_____

_____

_____

_____

6. What class, conference, book, or podcast helped you improve as a leader in the last year and why?

_____

_____

_____

_____

_____

CHAPTER 6

Create a Clear Vision

> Greatness starts with a clear vision of the future.
>
> —Simon Sinek

Your friend just invited you to a birthday party that's on the other side of town at a venue you aren't familiar with. You have the address, but you don't know where it is or how to get there. What do you do?

If you answered that you would plug it into Google Maps, or Waze or some other navigational app, then you are with over 75 percent of the population. Why do we use these apps? First, because they are super easy and convenient. But second, because they provide a clear path of direction—how to best and easily get to our destination. Without a plan, we have no direction, and neither does our team. One of the largest groups of individuals that I have had the luxury of coaching over the years are real estate agents. I would often get new prospects wanting to hire me because they wanted to start a team and didn't know how. We certainly have a great blueprint for starting and running successful teams, but it always starts with asking, "How are your current systems?" More times than not, they don't have any systems. They just know what to do in their head. Nothing written down, and no true step-by-step processes to follow for their daily and transactional tasks. When I discover this, it becomes the first thing we work on before hiring a single person to their team. No one wants to be on a team or working at a company where they don't truly have a blueprint to be successful.

Think of it this way: if I need to hire a front desk admin for my company, I can certainly find one who has held the position at other companies and has a strong background with that exact title on their resume from past employers. But how I want the job done versus their how managers or leaders at their past employer wanted it done could be much different. We need to spell out a system or plan so that we are clear with expectations once I hire them.

Let me give you an idea of how different one job to next can be, despite the title for the job being the same.

Whenever someone entered the office, I wanted my front desk admin to essentially stop what they were doing, look up at the person entering, smile, and say, "Welcome, how may I help you?" Even when it was another employee. Why? Because I wanted our workplace to be a happy place, and the first impression each day for our employees can be critical to their attitude or performance. In fact, I had some other colleagues at their office even title this position the Director of First Impressions.

Also, how do you answer the phone? Do you just answer and say, "Hello, this is ABC Company"? Or do you have a specific way you want people answering the phone? A dialogue, if you will. So we can see from just these two small examples of one person's job how confusion can happen when there isn't a clear vision for what that job looks like. In fact, I know managers who have disciplined or even written up employees because they were expected to just figure it out and when what they were doing didn't match the supervisor's expectation, it became a problem. I've shared this before, but conflict only arises when expectations differ.

Individual understanding of one's job and duties is reflective of one of the elements I wanted to discuss about having a clear vision. We must have a job description and a game plan or training schedule to ensure that each employee is properly trained on the front end as to what their expectation will be for their specific job function.

The other element of having a clear vision is more foundational to the company or your department. In fact, even before hiring that front desk admin, we need to be clear on the type of person we even want to hire. This involves having a well-thought-out MVVB (mission, vision, values, beliefs). Every company, and even each department, should have this if they hope to hire and maintain top talent.

The mission statement will define who your current client is and what you do to serve them. Typically, the mission statement is nonaspirational.

Visions statements are the more aspirational ones. They tend to make clear who your ideal client is, which may not be who you currently have as a customer, which is why it's aspirational. It also will include who you want to become in the process and who you want to be for them. Even if you aren't that person or company today. Here's an example of a vision statement from a fictitious roofing company: "We strive to have extremely loyal customers who visit us multiple times per year and are advocates for us. We are determined to be the number one roofing company in the entire market. We have knowledgeable staff who only perform at the highest level possible and with only positive energy when working." You can see that the statement uses words like "strive" because we aren't there yet. Obviously, we aren't currently number one either, which is why that goal is also inserted into the vision. Stating that you only want knowledgeable staff who perform at the highest level and have positive energy gives you direction when hiring. Once you clearly define your target audience and your target staff, you have directions to go with marketing for business and interviewing when looking for new employees.

Core values are extremely important to set the tone of what sort of things are important to the company or department. They should embody exactly what you stand for and who you desire to be. In my opinion, you should not have more than eight but no less than probably four. Our core values, for your reference, were

- Community impact: We desire to give back to the communities we serve and that support us.

- Fun: The job can be challenging at times and even stressful, which is why we must embrace being goofy at times.

- Personal growth: If you aren't growing, you're dying. Industries change quickly and tools change frequently. We must embrace the concept of consistent learning.

- Enthusiasm: We have the ability to choose our attitude each day, so let's show excitement for what we get to do.

- Habit driven: More is accomplished when you find
ways to be consistent. You can create good habits but
also bad ones. We choose to embrace good work habits
that support our company's mission and vision.

We changed them over time to accommodate the growing
company and new insights. Other examples you'll see for
core values are dependability, integrity, honesty, efficiency,
perseverance, service to others, passion, and respect.

When going through the process of selecting these for your
company, you can find many more options by simply Googling
"core values." James Clear, author of the amazing book *Atomic
Habits*, also has a great list on his website at jamesclear.com/
core-values.

Whatever you choose for your company or department,
create a short definition so that others in the organization will
be able to easily understand why you embrace the core values
you chose.

Beliefs are almost like affirmations. Things you print
and keep around the office to have others see. It helps keep
employees on track and moving forward, even when things
aren't going great. Some examples of beliefs:

- Conflict only happens when expectations differ.

- Your positive attitude will be reflected back to you
when your coworkers see it.

- Mistakes happen. When they do, make it right and
make it better.

I remember the first time creating the MVVB for my real estate brokerage, I had an expert on the topic invest eight hours of their time, all in one day, to help me hammer it out. They stood at a dry-erase board and wrote while I sat in a chair and threw words out to them. It is a painstaking process, but when done right, it can revolutionize the future of your business or department. For me, once I was done, I realized we had several individuals working with us who should've never been hired to begin with. We had a high turnover that year as we transitioned to following our mission, vision, core values, and beliefs. Two years later, we doubled our size and sales. How?

Having a clear vision for your business will allow you to truly think about what you want and don't want for your company, and also who you want and don't want. I compare this process to building a home. With a new home, you must have house plans so that you know the size, look, and number of bathrooms and bedrooms. Then, once you figure that part out, you can start with a solid foundation so that the structure can be supported properly and doesn't tumble down. Your mission, vision, core values, and beliefs will be the foundation for your business or department. Without a well-thought-out one that your team gets behind, your business will crumble.

Everyone needs to be on the same page once you have that MVVB. It should be a focus in office meetings, you should add posters about it on the walls of your business, and you should ensure they remain hyper focused on the importance of why you have the MVVB. It should be brought up in meetings frequently. We used to have our people read the MVVB aloud in these meetings. My most recent example of showing my team how extremely important core values are to our company and the future success of it was creating core value awards. Each year we would give an award to the individual in the company who best embodied each specific core value. Our people loved this friendly competition. We would even name nominees to give recognition to others who also embodied that core value but maybe didn't quite win it for that particular year.

By doing these types of things, you show your team how important it is to keep embracing the company mission, vision, core values, and beliefs. If the team sees how important these are to you, they will back them as well. In time, you will achieve the mission, and the vision will happen. It also keeps them in front of you by maintaining a deep focus on them throughout the year and allowing your team to call you or the company out if you aren't living up to them. With any luck, you'll find yourself having to redo your vision every few years, which is a sign of having the right focus in place for proper achievement.

If you have an existing mission and vision statement, one test you can give yourself is to ask your staff if they know what it is. We have found in our research that less than 40 percent of employees know what their company's mission or vision even is. This is very sad, because how can those employees help move the company toward achieving goals if they don't even know them? Hence the importance of getting the MVVB in front of your people often.

An article published by THM Agency found that over 90 percent of businesses that had well-defined mission statements achieve growth and profits that surpass industry averages. The same article shared how 65 percent of employees at firms with strong mission statements express a passion for their work, compared to only 32 percent at other workplaces.

In addition, this same article mentions how 84 percent of millennials prioritize finding meaning in their work, and 83 percent of Gen Z carefully weigh a company's mission before applying for a job. Millennials are 5.3 times more likely to remain with an employer if they feel a profound connection to the company's mission and purpose. There are also strong stats around the motivation of staff from these same companies, which I will share in a later chapter.

Amazing business leader Peter Drucker says, "A business is not defined by its name, statutes, or articles of incorporation. It is defined by the business mission. Only a clear definition of the mission and purpose of the organization makes possible clear and realistic business objectives."

Action Steps for "Create a Clear Vision"

1. What is your company or department's MVVB? If you don't have one, jot down some notes as you start to create this foundational piece for your company.

    a. Mission

    _____

    _____

    _____

    b. Vision

    _____

    _____

    _____

c. Core Values

_____

_____

_____

d. Beliefs

_____

_____

_____

2. If you have an existing MVVB, revisit it and decide if it needs to be redone.

_____

_____

_____

3. What is the deadline for completing this for your company?

_____

_____

*Turn the Dial Coaching offers training for your leadership team on creating a strong MVVB for your company. If you would like to learn more about hiring them to help you with this, please go to www.turnthedialcoaching.com/mvvb.

The Empathic Leader

> Leadership is about empathy. It is about having the ability to relate to and connect with people for the purpose of inspiring and empowering their lives.
>
> —Oprah Winfrey, TV personality, author, philanthropist

Empathic came up frequently as a leadership trait that employees seek. This makes a ton of sense to me, both as someone who is a leader that delivers on empathic feelings and as someone who has worked for others and sought it out.

What is empathic? For those who don't know, Cambridge Dictionary has the meaning as "having the ability to imagine how someone else feels." I have shared on many occasions that I have had battles, on and off for years, with depression. When someone finds out about my mental health struggles, they're sometimes saddened that I had to go through this. This is an example of being empathic. Having the ability to understand what I'm going through, and then empathizing with it. No one is asking you to feel the exact same way by being empathic. Really, it's a matter of not just saying, "Oh, that sucks. I'm sorry you're going through that," but rather expressing, in your own emotion, the pain and realization of what they are going through. In this example, I'm not desiring others to feel depression, but rather to seek to understand what depression feels like to me.

Harvard Business Review (HBR) releases some of the most amazing books on topics designed to help you in many areas of business. They did an entire series on emotional intelligence, and one of the six books is titled *Empathy*. The first chapter is written by an amazing expert in the field, Daniel Goleman, who has authored many books, including the bestseller *Emotional Intelligence*. He talks about the "empathy triad," which goes like this:

- Cognitive empathy: the ability to understand another person's perspective
- Emotional empathy: the ability to feel what someone else feels
- Empathic concern: the ability to sense what another person needs from you

As you can imagine, we can write an entire book just on this topic. To fully understand all three and, as a leader, get yourself in a position to better work with your people as a result, it takes time.

If you decide to dive deeper into this topic, I recommend picking up *Empathy* from HBR's Emotional Intelligence Series. But let me also give you a real-life example, just to set the tone for this chapter.

Imagine you have an employee whose mom suddenly passed away and they are asking for time off. Being short-staffed because an employee needs personal time is not ideal and puts stress on the business. But if you truly care about your people, you must be empathetic to whatever they are going through. I like to imagine I am in their shoes. How would I feel if I got word that my mom just passed? Devastated. Tears would start flowing. And in that moment, my job would be one of the last things I'm thinking about. So, in moments like this, we must think from their perspective. It will help us as leaders better create a plan to allow this employee to handle whatever family affairs they need. We need to take the stance of "I've got you. We'll be fine here. Family is most important. Go be with them." This immediately shows you can understand that this is a painful moment in their life, and you support them during this tough season. If you can do this. Don't panic about being short-staffed. Maybe even send flowers and a sympathetic card to the family—that's how you show care as a leader.

I had a friend of mine, Jenifer Morin from Virginia, share her exact story on this topic, which I think demonstrated this point perfectly. She said, "Just two weeks after I started at Gateway, my mother was diagnosed with stage 4 cancer. Scott understood the gravity of the situation and immediately expressed his empathy and support. He told me to take as much time as I needed to be with my mom and assist her with her appointments. Sadly, my mother passed away three months later. During this incredibly difficult time, Scott (and the rest of my coworkers) again showed sincere empathy by encouraging me to take as much time off as I needed to be with my family and handle all necessary arrangements. I only took two days off, but still, it was offered. He went above and beyond by sending a full meal to my home one evening to help with dinner, easing one small burden during a challenging time. He also ensured my workload was covered when I was out, so I didn't have to worry about work on top of my grief. This gesture was so appreciated! This experience showed me that a leader who shows empathy and supports their employees from the beginning and during difficult times builds a strong foundation of trust and respect. When I share this story, people understand my loyalty to Scott, as he has shown me empathy and respect from the very beginning."

Just to be clear, the Scott mentioned in this example is Scott MacDonald, who owns a large RE/MAX brokerage in the Washington, DC, area. I know Scott personally, and he has had significant growth in his company. This does not surprise me because of how I see him operate, as outlined briefly in this one example.

The stories that were shared with me about the importance of a leader possessing empathy were too numerous to put in this book, but I did have a few other comments I wanted to share from my research on this topic.

"It is important for me to work for someone who has the ability to be compassionate," said one respondent on the topic of having an empathic and caring leader. Said a different way, she doesn't want to work at a place that only sees her as a number and not a human being.

Another respondent shared a story that again demonstrates empathy. Kelsey Sanders from Michigan said, "When I was working in corporate, I broke up with a long-time boyfriend and it was devasting. So I wanted to adopt a dog. I found one and they would only hold him for me until closing time (six p.m.), but my shift was until six thirty. I talked to my boss, who was a dog lover and very sympathetic during my breakup, and she said if our coworker would cover for me, I could leave early and go adopt the dog. It all worked out and seven years later, that little guy still brings me comfort and joy. And she still asks about him ☺ Seems like a small thing, but her empathy to my emotional situation and what I needed at that time was huge. Life-changing, even."

Do individuals actually choose their places of employment based on things unrelated to the job? Absolutely. I can't tell you how many interviews I conducted where at the end I asked, "Any questions that you have for me?" And they would ask me how we gave back to the communities my company was involved in or what sort of volunteer work I did. I have found that interviews are a great place to learn what people are looking for in you as a leader and in your company. I got asked this question so often that we made community driven a core value for our company.

If your company or department can create regular ways of giving back throughout the year, it helps keep the empathy flowing in the company and with you as a leader in the company. One of the largest nonprofits that we supported over the years was Children's Miracle Network Hospitals. If you aren't familiar with this amazing organization, it was started by Marie Osmond, John Schneider, Mick Shannon, and Joe Lake in 1983. Over the years they have provided funding to over 158 hospitals across the country and raised more than $7 billion in funding. The stories that are shared in videos and on stages at conferences I have attended will pull your heartstrings. Personally, my wife and I don't have kids, but I am absolutely empathetic to what these kids and their families are going through, sometimes life-threatening illnesses and diseases. Try to put yourself in the kid's shoes. How are they feeling? Scared? Worried? What about the parents? Often, they are wondering how they are going to pay the medical expenses for these expensive procedures that need to be done to save their child's life. Trying to understand their perspective.

We believed in the mission of Children's Miracle Network Hospitals so much that we created a 501(c)(3) nonprofit to help raise additional funds for them, which we have done successfully for many years now and still run this organization today.

Why do I share all of this? Because I truly believe that if you put yourself or your company in a position to support nonprofits like Children's Miracle Network Hospitals, you too will hear the real struggles that life puts on individuals and animals every year. You will become a more caring and more empathic individual if you can find yourself actively participating in these organizations. One way to do this is by joining a nonprofit board of directors.

Nonprofits always need community leaders to help them make key decisions and raise much-needed funding for their programs. By being on boards of nonprofits, I learn more about these struggles firsthand, and typically you share these board positions with other leaders of other companies around town. I've learned a lot from my fellow board members about leadership. Hence, joining a board can benefit you in another way by helping you improve your leadership skills.

Occasionally as leaders we may find ourselves having to coach our employees, maybe on mistakes they made or improper behavior. One of my respondents, Kate Rossart, shared some great phrases her prior supervisor would use, like "tell me why" or "tell me more about . . ." or "help me understand." "And then he would share his opinions and thoughts after he understood why I did what I did." These are great words to keep in your back pocket if you struggle with being more empathic toward staff.

As my direct supervisor in the air force, John Stimer, once told me, "Empathy is multilayered. It shows a leader cares about the people they are leading as well as rapport building. All of this leads to a more cohesive work environment."

Not everyone has the same strengths. Not everyone has the same background or resume. Understanding this and meeting each individual where they are shows a great deal of empathy. In fact, I'll end this chapter cementing this point with a quote from one of my favorite mentors, motivational speakers, and business experts.

> As a leader, you should always start with where people are before you try to take them to where you want them to go.
>
> —Jim Rohn

Action Steps for "The Empathic Leader"

1. What is your main takeaway from this chapter?

_____

_____

_____

2. In what ways do you currently show empathy toward others? If you don't feel you currently do, how can you start?

_____

_____

_____

3. What nonprofit organizations are you currently involved in? If you aren't involved with any, what nonprofits can you see yourself becoming more active with?

_____

_____

_____

4. Do you currently meet your people where they are, or do you expect them to all be up to speed in the same areas? Journal some thoughts about this here:

_____

_____

_____

_____

_____

CHAPTER 8

An, Honest, Authentic, Transparent Leader Wins

> I think the currency of leadership is transparency. You've got to be truthful. I don't think you should be vulnerable every day, but there are moments where you've got to share your soul and conscience with people and show them who you are, and not be afraid of it.
>
> —Howard Schultz, former CEO of Starbucks

Would you prefer to work for someone who is authentic or fake? What about a leader who lies versus one who tells the truth? How about one who shares behind the scenes to give you perspective versus a leader who hides what's going on, leaving you confused and maybe even disgruntled? Do these questions seem ridiculous to you? Well, these leaders exist in many organizations. In fact, you may be one and not truly understand you are. How? Well, sometimes we have to deal with difficult circumstances, and our instant reaction is that we need to keep this information confidential. Obviously you can't let staff know that the company is financially a disaster, right?

Over my more than thirty years of managing and leading individuals, I have at times been the guy hiding information I felt to be too sensitive for staff. I have kept secrets from them thinking that I was doing the company and them a favor. But looking back on those times, I would have done things differently, and in recent years I have.

Though most of my companies have been highly profitable over the years, those companies certainly weren't free from troubling times. During the Great Recession, I owned a real estate brokerage that had just opened. What a time to be in real estate. And not in a good way. I was forced to move my office location three times in three years because I simply could not afford my lease payment. Each time I decided that it was important for my people to know it was for financial reasons. "The economy has not been favorable to the real estate market, as you know, and so in an effort for us to stay afloat as a company, we need to move locations again." This was scary for me to say. Embarrassing even. But absolutely needed for transparency. Often our people can feel when things aren't right anyways. So don't sugarcoat it. Be transparent and you'll find a deeper sense of loyalty, which I certainly gained. In fact, twelve years after the Great Recession ended, I had all my people still. I've since sold that brokerage. The fact that my people stood by me through those tough times also led me to have a stronger sense of loyalty and dedication to helping them grow and become more successful.

I've also found admitting that things aren't always peachy leads to a sense of you being more human. Truth is, we aren't robots. We can't always be on, and we can't always have things going amazingly. At some point, something will break. Profits will go down. Sales might suffer. During these times, we will be tested. My survey participants stated in great numbers that they prefer to work for leaders who are honest and transparent about the situation when this happens. In *Are You a Manager or a Leader?* I have a chapter called "Leading through Challenging Times." I encourage you to read that first book in my series on leadership if you need additional guidance on leading when things go wrong. I give many examples of things I did, of journaling I did, which then helped me when we were challenged years later during COVID-19.

But what about being an authentic leader? What does this even mean? Well, Google it and you will find many varying answers, but the answer that resonated with me most is that it is a management style in which people act in a real, genuine, and sincere way that is true to who they are as individuals.

When my wife and I owned a RE/MAX franchise, we once had a CEO, Adam Contos, who showed me all about the importance of transparency and authenticity. He was truly leading other leaders, and I was one to follow suit. He did it mostly using video. Live videos at that. Many times, unedited. You got to see Adam raw and with faults. You got to see the great and any imperfections. This made him human. And when you are human as a leader, you become very approachable, as Adam was to those who knew him. Also, even though I didn't see Adam in person often because he held such a high role with the company, I felt like I knew him. Through the raw videos he always did. That's another reason why we should be making more videos as leaders. Start with ones of care, like we discussed earlier. Then eventually move some video to other avenues that may be a bit more public, like social media. This will certainly help accelerate the feeling of being approachable. Just make sure that they are not overtly scripted. Those types of videos tend to make us seem fake and almost robotic.

In my real estate coaching, I am often training salespeople on how to better have conversations that almost guarantee a higher level of conversion on leads and objection handling. We even give them several examples of dialogues to use to have better success. But what is a dialogue? It is an idea of how to say something best that most commonly has been found to work. But I also train that you don't want to just say the dialogue verbatim. You want to understand the key principles of the dialogue, but then make it your own. Just because Jimmy Bob perfected a way to sell more widgets doesn't mean the exact same dialogue will work for you too. After all, Jimmy Bob may have an accent. He may use vocabulary that you never use. If you say the dialogue like Jimmy Bob, you will likely sound fake, and it can hurt your chances of getting that client's business. Instead, understand those key principles that Jimmy Bob tries to convey, and then make them your own. It will come across much more authentic, and you will earn the trust of the client so well that it can lead to even more business or referrals. Because it was authentically you.

HBR has a book on authentic leadership, and in it they discuss a study of when companies ended up in the news for bad things they have done or scandals they've been part of. It was interesting to read how when a CEO apologized publicly through video and did it with a smile on their face, stock prices went down. Possibly because the average person assumed they weren't sincere in their apology. Versus the CEOs who apologized and looked sad about what happened. Their stock prices rose. Authentic. That's what people demand. And when we are true to ourselves and honest, only good things will happen for us and our companies.

> True leadership stems from individuality that is honestly and sometimes imperfectly expressed. Leaders should strive for authenticity over perfection.
>
> —Sheryl Sandberg, former CEO of Facebook

Action Steps for "Honest, Authentic, Transparent Leaders Win"

1. Reflect on when things weren't perfect in your organization. What is something you feel like you sugarcoated or maybe withheld from your people?

_____

_____

_____

_____

2. What is something you can do today to show your staff more transparency or honesty?

_____

_____

_____

_____

3. Do you have the courage to ask your staff if they feel you are an authentic and transparent leader? What did they say if you asked them this question?

_____

_____

_____

_____

4. What does being authentic mean in your life?

_____

_____

_____

_____

CHAPTER 9

Motivated and Inspired Workers Will Get Behind You

> Leaders must be close enough to relate to others, but far enough ahead to motivate them.
>
> —John C. Maxwell, bestselling author in leadership and business

You may ask yourself, *Is it really important to motivate others? I'm not a motivational speaker, so how do I even try to do this with my staff, and why should I?* Great questions, for sure. I have so many reasons why, but let's start by defining what motivation even is. I love the definition by Wikipedia, which is "an internal state that propels individuals to engage in goal-driven activities." Like their job. Ask yourself, *Why do your workers do their job?* Let's explore a couple of answers.

1. They need to pay their bills at home. Yes, the answer, if you asked, can be that simple. But if that's all it is, they will always have a wandering eye for another job that may be more impactful or fun.

Or they may answer . . .

2. Because if I don't do my job, I'll get fired and I need this job. Not a great answer either, correct? It makes me believe that this person works under intimidation versus inspiration.

Now let's assume you've created that mission and vision statement we discussed earlier. Let me show how simple words can absolutely transform a workforce. I have taught for many years the importance of having a unique selling proposition (USP). This is in an effort to stand out from our competition. But let's stay on the track of why workers show up to work.

Instead of my examples above, let me share with you one of my favorite shoe company's mission statement and how they achieve it. This is TOMS shoes:

TOMS's mission is to improve lives through business by creating good-looking products, partnering with others, and conducting business ethically. TOMS's main ways of achieving this mission include:

- Donating shoes: TOMS matches every pair of shoes purchased with a donation of a pair of shoes to a child in need. TOMS also provides different types of shoes based on the seasons and terrain of the communities in need.

- Funding nonprofits: TOMS donates one-third of its profits to nonprofits through cash grants and partnerships. TOMS's main focus is funding nonprofits that provide mental health resources, education, employment, and gun violence prevention programs.

- Other initiatives: TOMS has also helped restore the sight of 150,000 people in ten countries by providing prescription glasses, medical treatment, and sight-saving surgeries.

Back to the article I mentioned earlier from THM Agency where they mention that organizations with robust mission statements have 63 percent of their staff feeling motivated in their work versus just 31 percent in companies without strong missions.

Can you see how if I worked at TOMS I may have a different answer when someone asks why I work for them? My company donates a pair of shoes for each pair we sell. I'm going to work with a deeper purpose. I feel more motivated, even if I do the same job someone at another shoe company without the same mission does. Hopefully this makes sense. If you would like a further dive into the importance of strong mission and vision statements for your business, check out the article by Harvard Business Review titled *The Founder of Toms Reimagining the Company's Mission*. The article is actually written by TOMS' founder Blake Mycoskie. He explains the rapid success of startup to $300 million in revenue and how leading with purpose over process was a huge part of TOMS' early success.

If it doesn't make sense, let me give one more example. There are several nonprofits that exist where there are board members who do work for the organization, but they never get paid. Now what do you think motivates them to do this? It's not the pay. There are typically no benefits either. It's usually the mission of the organization. I cofounded a nonprofit called Making Miracles Support Foundation, which raises money for Children's Miracles Network Hospitals each year. We have the privilege of providing much-needed funding to families of children who can't afford the life-changing or, in some cases, lifesaving procedures they are getting. Without us and other organizations raising these funds, what would happen? Well, I choose to never know that answer. Our auction committee invests countless hours outside of their normal jobs and family functions to pull off our annual fundraising auction. Motivation. It is deeply needed, and your people might be looking for some.

But how can we get motivated? There are several ways to accomplish this. One of the top ones I've seen has been attending industry conferences. Most industries have conferences, and most conferences bring in good keynote speakers who maybe aren't in your industry, but they were brought in to motivate you.

Have you ever been to a conference where at the end of the keynote session you were pumped up and ready to take on the world? If the answer is no, then you're going to the wrong conferences. Or maybe you haven't been to any conferences, and that certainly should change. My primary business focus today is in the personal development and coaching space, so I have the luxury of attending several amazing conferences with these types of speakers and also, at times, being asked to be the keynote speaker and inspire the crowd myself. On average I attend three different conferences each year on varying topics relevant to improving myself.

In my experience, many attendees often take tons of notes that they then bring back home and do nothing with. They leave so inspired, with great new ideas, but fall flat with execution.

In the *New York Times* bestselling book *The 12 Week Year*, for which I am a certified trainer, Brian Moran and Michael Lennington mention how lack of execution is the main reason people don't accomplish things in life. In fact, it's mentioned on the first page of the book. They say that the greatest predictor of your future are your daily actions.

What do your daily habits look like? One of the masters at motivation is Zig Ziglar, who says, "People often say that motivation doesn't last. Well, neither does bathing—that's why we recommend it daily."

This begs the questions: What do you do daily to keep yourself in the right headspace? What keeps you pumped up? Then my next question would be, what do you do to pump up and motivate your employees? They need it too, or they get bored. They get uninspired. They may start exploring other options and eventually leave you and your company. This reminds me of the William Johnsen quote, "If it is to be, it is up to me." We must be the solution to stay motivated for ourselves and offer elements of motivation for our staff.

One way to accomplish this is through regular recognition. But not fake recognition just because. We live in a world where participation trophies are a thing. How? I believe in recognizing a job well done or good results. But not just because the employee might feel jealous or sad if they don't get recognized. Imagine you recognize every one of your team of ten, even though most of the work was performed by just two of those ten. How would those two feel? Like you don't recognize this disparity in work. Eventually they will leave you, and you'll be left with the bottom feeders in your organization. I'm not insinuating that we throw the others under the bus, but certainly those top two individuals deserve credit or recognition. This will keep them motivated and inspire them to do more great work for you and the company, and hopefully, if done properly, it will inspire others to want to work better and be like those top two.

That said, in a world of heavy social media, I often hear from coaching clients that they see all of these amazing feats and levels of achievement from their competition. They often wonder how they get to that level. Well for one I remind them that they are in coaching and in time I can get them there. But also, I remind them that we cannot compare ourselves to others. We must compare ourselves to us. To ourselves. If you get 10 percent better each year, imagine where you'll be in ten years. You'll be a whole different person. This is why my wife and I named our company Turn the Dial Coaching. Even though the average person today wants instant gratification and the roadmap to instant success, we understand that the path to success is having a plan, being consistent with that plan, and growing a little each year. This why Darren Hardy wrote the *New York Times* bestseller *The Compound Effect*, as discussed previously. Speaking of Darren Hardy, he has something called Darren Daily. It is a quick motivational, pump-you-up video that Darren himself sends to you each workday. We're talking five minutes or less. Anyone has time for this, and I highly encourage you to jump in on this community. He also has a private Facebook page called Be the Exception, which is a community of like-minded people, many of them leaders, who help inspire one another and keep each other motivated.

Also, we are building a community of our own on social media, so be sure to join our Facebook group, The Inspiring Leader Group with Scott Comey, as well.

Sam Walton, founder of Walmart, knew how incredibly important keeping his staff motivated was to his business. He says this, "Outstanding leaders go out of their way to boost the self-esteem of their personnel. If people believe in themselves, it's amazing what they can accomplish."

Action Steps for "Motivated and Inspired Workers Will Get Behind You"

1. In what ways do you currently recognize staff?

   _____

   _____

   _____

   _____

2. What is a new way you can inspire and motivate staff that you currently aren't doing?

   _____

   _____

   _____

   _____

3. Join Darren Daily (darrendaily.com).

4. Join The Inspiring Leader Series with Scott Comey, our Facebook group, for more inspiration.

CHAPTER 10

Be the Leader Your People Desire

> A true leader has the confidence to stand alone, the courage to make tough decisions, and the compassion to listen to the needs of others. He does not set out to be a leader, but becomes one by the equality of his actions and the integrity of his intent.
>
> —General Douglas MacArthur

I remember reading a short biography of General Douglas MacArthur for the first time. I felt very much like I had not done enough in my life. If you want to feel inept in your resume, check out General MacArthur's. Wow. To put it in perspective, let me showcase a few of his highlights. General MacArthur was chief of staff of the army in the 1930s; he was nominated for the Medal of Honor three times and received it for his work in the Philippines campaign. He also was the first captain of the United States Military Academy at West

Point, where he graduated top of his class. In addition, he was awarded the Distinguished Service Cross for his work during World War I and awarded the Silver Star Medal seven times. Fast forward several years where in 1945 he accepted the official surrender of Japan during World War II and from that point to 1951, he was the effective ruler of Japan during the occupation. This represents maybe half of all he has on his resume. Very impressive leader.

There have not been too many leaders who have had the immense levels of stress yet extreme amount of success as this amazing war hero. Luckily, as I mentioned in the previous chapter, it's not healthy for our soul to compare ourselves to others. That said, the quote above from General MacArthur tells me all I need to know about how to be a great leader.

He touches on a few elements that we can all learn from.

1. "Confidence to stand alone"—we must be responsible for everything within our control, which sometimes feels like a very lonely place to be.

2. "Have courage to make tough decisions"—there will be many times, as a leader, that we will be faced with decisions that scare us. But it shouldn't stop us from proceeding with making them. To me, that's courage—when you don't know what the outcome might be but are trusting that it will be the right one.

3. "Compassion to listen to the needs of others"—we discussed earlier about the importance of caring for the people within your employ and also having empathy for them in times when it's needed. Listening is such an important skill that, as leaders, we must master.

4. "You'll become a leader by the equality of your actions and integrity of your intent"—this thought is why we have an entire chapter on honesty, authenticity, and transparency. We must demonstrate firsthand our expectations, set clear visions for the positions of the people we lead, be honest with our actions, and be transparent with why things are the way they are.

These principles clearly sum up the chapters of the book and the thoughts and comments that we solicited from our surveys and research. The people you lead are willing to do what's asked and do it with their best efforts. But will they? The answer rests in whether you are a manager or a leader. Again, I clearly define this difference in *Are You a Manager or a Leader?* but in summary: Managers follow orders, check performance, offer corrective action based on performance management, and follow company policies set by others.

But when defining a leader, it is slightly different in that it is the act of getting people (employees, soldiers, etc.) to follow the direction you lay out for them. Good leaders can get their people to do amazing things, because they want to and not because they have to. They see a clear picture of what their actions can provide or what the end result can be, because the example has been laid out in a vision by their leader. The leader has painted a great picture of what success looks like. Success of a project, of a business, of winning a battle.

Leaders tend to inspire through their efforts—leading by example—and being the ones who set the expectations themselves. They look in the mirror before deciding to manage performance and inspire great results.

Employees want to be led. They don't tend to want to be managed. Any manager can become a leader. The choice is theirs. If you haven't read any of the Ken Blanchard books on leadership, check them out. There are very short, skinny books that are an easy read. In his book *The Leadership Pill*, he and his coauthor Marc Muchnick mention how leadership is not something you do *to* people. It's something you do *with* people. They mention how if I respect my employees, then I face them. I ask for their advice and input on certain decisions. In a low-respect environment, I don't care what you think, which means I don't respect your thoughts. Which means I have my back to you. That's why we need to work *with* our employees and involve them on occasion in decisions.

So what do employees want their leaders to look like? Well, many of the clues have been shared in the book. But it all starts with trust. I have often said that we need to seek to be trusted by staff and worry later about whether they will like you. It has been said that it's better to be trusted than liked as a leader.

Let me offer a quick example. Let's say you are in the military and getting ready to step on to a very dangerous battlefield. Would you prefer to do it with a leader you trust but maybe don't personally like? Or with the leader you like but maybe don't have respect or trust for? I know what my answer would be. I'm not saying it doesn't hurt one's ego to not be liked. But there is a difference between not being liked and being hated. So if your mind went to *I don't want my people to hate me*, you're not alone. Neither do I. But are you okay if they just don't like you, but trust you as their leader? That's the key difference. And this isn't to say you can't be both liked and trusted. I am just stating that we need to shoot for trust first.

This becomes challenging for the people pleaser that so many leaders are. They want to be friends even with their staff. I have seen this backfire too often. Going for like versus respect won't be sustainable. Especially if you get to the point of having to coach them on something they may have done wrong.

It is alarming to me the high percentage of workers that statistically are not happy at work. In fact, according to Gallup's 2022 State of the Global Workplace report, as high as 85 percent of the world's full-time workers may be unhappy at work. As if this isn't alarming enough, 50 percent of US workers share that they are stressed at work. These are the types of things we as leaders must know about so that we can address them within our own organizations and work to improve them. One of my good friends and TEDx speaker Greg Kettner has even made this his life's work, having founded a company called WorkHappy with a podcast named the same. Greg goes to companies and talks with them about happiness and sadness and tells great stories to help improve whatever circumstances might be going on in somebody's life at the moment. After I hired Greg to come speak to my company, which I had thought was full of highly motivated and happy people, I was shocked by the results. They said, "Thanks so much, I needed that." Some were moved to tears. And as their leader, I had no idea. I learned a valuable lesson on this day. I wasn't asking the *right* questions of my people when we chatted. Or I didn't notice the silent cues that could've alerted me to their sadness.

So again, take the lessons taught in this book to heart. There is input from so many people, tons of books, many podcasts, and some training programs. Learn from my mistakes and from the examples shared by my survey participants about what they like in their bosses and what they don't like.

> Be the kind of leader that people would follow voluntarily, even if you had no title or position.
>
> —Brian Tracy, bestselling author and business expert

Action Steps for "Be the Leader Your People Desire"

1. What do your people want most? If you don't know, ask or survey them.

_____

_____

_____

_____

2. What do you look for in the leaders above you? Are these things you provide for your own people? If not, can you start?

_____

_____

_____

_____

_____

3. On a scale of 1 to 10 (where 1 is you don't listen at all and 10 is that you are an amazing listener), how would you rank your listening skills with your employees?

_____

_____

a. How do you increase that more toward a 10?

_____

_____

_____

_____

_____

AFTERWORD

> A leader is anyone who takes responsibility for finding the potential in people and processes and has the courage to develop that potential.
>
> —Brené Brown

Brené Brown is certainly an expert in the area of leadership, and her books have risen to bestseller status multiple times. I tend to follow the advice of great writers and businesspeople, and Brené is certainly both of those. I love her quote here because it offers a simple thought: focus on the good in people versus the bad. I think all too often leaders tend to focus on what their employees don't do versus what they do right. They criticize too hard the lack of perfection and don't think about long-term growth and potential. If you switch your thinking to focus this way, it will become instantly clear by those you lead. She also mentions in the same quote about focusing on finding potential in processes. I take this as meaning to never be content with the way things are done.

I have always followed this school of thinking, and it has served me well in the CEO roles I've held and chairman positions at nonprofits alike. Technology changes and new tools become available. Not to mention that if you are constantly seeking feedback from your customers and staff, you will get advice from them on a better way to do things.

It has been quite the process of writing this leadership book from the perspective of those being led, and it has been enlightening for me. I hope that you too found some golden nuggets on ways to improve your current leadership style. None of us should ever feel like we are a perfect leader. We need to keep the mentality that we can always do better and raise the bar even higher. We should also never be afraid of someone else taking over our position, as you will stunt the growth of those below you and take away from the prospect of them seeing growth within your organization. And as you saw on the chart I shared earlier, that is one of the top reasons why people quit their jobs—no growth, or lack of growth or opportunities. Years ago, I managed and owned coffee shops. The assistant manager who reported directly to me was constantly being promoted from my store to go run a different store within the company. It would be easy to get frustrated by this sort of action, as I seemed to be always losing my best person. But instead, I focused on being happy for them versus bitter. It's turning the focus on them versus us. I will get another assistant manager, and you know what? I will train and develop them to be amazing, just like the one I'm losing.

That mentality led to me being sought after by employees looking for a fast track to promotion. They knew I did it well and wasn't afraid to eventually lose them when they got promoted. This helped the overall team morale, and we had the best group of employees for years as a result. A winning culture. That's what anyone on your team can hope for.

As you saw from the graphics I showed in the book, most employees aren't going to make their salary the primary reason for leaving. I think it's a cop-out that we assume things like low compensation or lack of benefits are the primary reasons why people quit. The leader themselves is number one on the list. If we can fix this and improve communication with our people, we can retain at a higher level. This doesn't mean we shouldn't be financially rewarding with raises or bonuses when appropriate, but it's just statistically not the most important thing to the average worker. Their leader and workplace culture are higher. If we are also patient when they make a mistake, it can help build long-term loyalty. I have made a few major mistakes in my career, some that have cost thousands to fix. I was very grateful when I found my leader was patient and retrained me versus an immediate write-up or worse, firing me. I have learned over the years that there are two types of leaders: those who intimidate, and those who inspire. No one wants to come to work scared, so let's stay away from intimidation. But inspiration they can get behind.

Now it's your turn to take the knowledge gained by reading this book and put it into actionable steps so that you can start transforming your own leadership levels. As I mentioned earlier about how oftentimes we attend conferences and take lots of notes but do nothing with the notes, people do the same with books. They dog-ear, they highlight, they take notes, and then they never go back, hoping what they've learned and read starts working for them through osmosis. Maybe you even did that with this book. But we know that execution is where it's at. Again, it's part of the reason *The 12 Week Year* was written and became a *New York Times* bestseller. Because people need better ways and better systems to execute at a higher level.

Fortunately for you, I've added action steps at the end of each chapter. Hopefully you answered those questions and wrote on those pages. If you did not, this is your chance to go back and do it. The first step in improving your leadership skills is to take a look at those action steps and complete them.

Also, check out the reading list we've included at the back of this book for some other ways to improve your skills. And then join our Facebook community, The Inspired Leader with Scott Comey, of other leaders all looking to share and improve their current leadership level. And if I can help in any way, please reach out directly to me.

scomey@turnthedialcoaching.com

Thank you so much for trusting that this book is what you needed. Thank you for allowing me to share some insight from those who are being led so that they may show us how we can be better and gain their trust and respect more.

If you have gotten even one good idea from this book, please share it with someone who can benefit from it. And if you have not read my first book in the series, please check out *Are You a Manager or a Leader?*

ACKNOWLEDGEMENTS

This book could not have been made possible without the help of numerous contributors. In the many surveys, posts, and questions I sent out, I received an overwhelming amount of content to help piece together this book. The list below represents people from around the United States, Canada, and many varying walks of life. Thank you to all who contributed.

Tony Rubleski, Michigan

Kate Rossart, Washington

Jody Black, Mississippi

Kelsey Sanders, Michigan

Shayla Deam, Missouri

Amanda Bocook, Washington

Shea Murphy, Colorado

Kathy Slack, Washington

Jenifer Morin, Virginia

Michelle Timmons
Hoyt, Illinois

Tiffinie Autio, Washington

Stacy Washburn Gillen, Indiana

Jody Scott, Washington

Wendy Coon, Michigan

Marci Miller, Washington

Abby Wilson, Michigan

Shannon Mehalik, California

Jonathan Lerche, New York

Andy Weiser, Florida

Dawn Shroba, South Carolina

Izabella Reid, Washington

John Stimer, Washington

Jeanette Jennings, California

Amanda LeVeck, Washington

Charlie Foxworth, Texas

Paul Graf, Washington

Angelene Ukena, Georgia

Karen Knickerbocker, Washington

Jim Reece, Washington

Paul Guyon, Michigan

Charlie Smith, Washington

Vania Bourdeau, Florida

Renee Comey, South Carolina

Anne Allen, Washington

Redfern, Arizona

Cynthia Caffrey, Washington

Aimee Anthony-Smith, Washington

DeDe Heggem, Arizona

Karie Anthony, Washington

Jessica Adams, Florida

Tina Leggett, Washington

Maureen Butwin, South Carolina

Mara Arnold, Washington

Wendi Hale, Washington

Aaron Moss, North Dakota

Heidi Root, Washington

Karin Ehrhorn, Washington

Rick Brandt, Virginia

Telishia Altis, Washington

Alesa Morales, South Carolina

Kari Zimmerman, Washington

Heather Goodman Penichet, Kentucky

Greg Ocken, Washington

Barry Halpern Jr, South Carolina

Cory Ehrhorn, Washington

Richelle Stephens, Washington

Stacey Davis-Militana, South Carolina

Dave Gardner, Washington

Sam Olson, Nevada

Christy Jones, Washington

Brenda Alfano, Washington

Renee Mangan, Oregon

Jeffrey Clark, Washington

Tyrone Davids, Toronto

Jack Berner, Washington

Christopher Dietz, Washington

John Stimer, Washington

Bob Koch, South Carolina

Dawn Wright, Washington

Lisa Lopez, Texas

Steve Autio, Washington

Samantha Alley, Oregon

Tim Haag, Idaho

Jack Markham, Washington

Michelle Caietta, South Carolina

Jermaine Hargrove, Washington

SCOTT'S RECOMMENDED READING LIST

There have been many books written on so many topics, and I continue to devour as many as I can each year to help myself grow in areas I need improvement. I could've easily made this list ten times the size it is, but sometimes too many decisions can stall progress and so I just picked some of my favorites for this list. Otherwise, it would've felt like going to the Cheesecake Factory—too many good choices that you don't know which one to go with.

If you have a read a great book that is not already on this list, I would love to hear from you. I'm always looking for some new options on good topics. You can connect with me at **scomey@turnthedialcoaching.com**. Enjoy!

Execution/Habits/Routines

- *The Miracle Morning* by Hal Elrod
- *The 12 Week Year: Get More Done in 12 Weeks than Others Do in 12 Months* by Brian P. Moran and Michael Lennington
- *Atomic Habits: An Easy & Proven Way to Build Good Habits & Break Bad Ones* by James Clear

- *Uncommon Accountability: A Radical New Approach to Greater Success and Fulfillment* by Brian P. Moran and Michael Lennington
- *The Slight Edge: Turning Simple Disciplines into Massive Success & Happiness* by Jeff Olson

Mindset/Determination/Achievement

- *The Emigrant Edge: How to Make It Big in America* by Brian Buffini
- *The Four Agreements: A Practical Guide to Personal Freedom* by Don Miguel Ruiz
- *Man's Search for Meaning* by Viktor E. Frankl
- *Change Your Thinking, Change Your Life: How to Unlock Your Full Potential for Success and Achievement* by Brian Tracy
- *Start with Why: How Great Leaders Inspire Everyone to Take Action* by Simon Sinek
- *The Compound Effect: Jumpstart Your Income, Your Life, Your Success* by Darren Hardy
- *Who Not How: The Formula to Achieve Bigger Goals Through Accelerating Teamwork* by Dan Sullivan and Dr. Benjamin Hardy
- *Grit: The Power of Passion and Perseverance* by Angela Duckworth
- *Rejection Proof: How I Beat Fear and Become Invincible Through 100 Days of Rejection* by Jia Jiang

- *The 5 Second Rule: Transform your Life, Work, and Confidence with Everyday Courage* by Mel Robbins

Getting More Done in the Time Allotted

- *Essentialism: The Disciplined Pursuit of Less* by Greg McKeown
- *Free to Focus: A Total Productivity System to Achieve More by Doing Less* by Michael Hyatt
- *Eat That Frog!: 21 Great Ways to Stop Procrastinating and Get More Done in Less Time* by Brian Tracy

Improving Communication

- *Human-Centered Communication: A Business Case Against Digital Pollution* by Ethan Beute and Stephen Pacinelli
- *Change Your Questions, Change Your Life: 10 Powerful Tools for Life and Work* by Marilee Adams

Other Great Leadership Books

- *Are You a Manager or a Leader?: How to Inspire Results Through Others* by Scott Comey
- *Everybody Wins: The Story and Lessons Behind RE/MAX* by Phil Harkins and Keith Hollihan
- *The Go-Giver Leader: A Little Story About What Matters Most in Business* by Bob Burg and John David Mann

- *The One Minute Manager* by Kenneth Blanchard and Spencer Johnson
- *Mind Capture: Leadership Lessons from Ten Trailblazers Who Beat the Odds and Influenced Millions* by Tony Rubleski
- *Now, Discover Your Strengths: The revolutionary Gallup program that shows you how to develop your unique talents and strengths* – and Those of the People You Manage by Marcus Buckingham and Donald O. Clifton
- *Swim! How a Shark, a Suckerfish, and a Parasite Teach You Leadership, Mentoring, and Next Level Success* by Walter Bond
- *Authentic Leadership: HBR Emotional Intelligence Series* by Harvard Business Review

AUTHOR BIO

Scott Comey has had incredible success in many varying business ventures over the years. He has had two books hit bestseller status, *Are You a Manager or a Leader?* and *Real Estate Fast Track*, a book he coauthored with Sam Olson. In addition to being an author, Scott is a coach, trainer, and speaker on the topic of business leadership and in the real estate industry. He owns and runs Turn the Dial Coaching and the podcast of the same name, is an entrepreneur, and holds two patents. Scott also started a 501(c)(3) nonprofit organization called Making Miracles Support Foundation. This organization is designed to support Children's Miracle Network Hospitals and Seattle Children's Hospital. Comey is also a former chairman of the board for Big Brothers Big Sisters of Snohomish County and has sat on multiple boards in the real estate industry and for other nonprofits. Scott and his wife are huge coffee and wine people, and love watching live music and going to concerts. They also enjoy living in Myrtle Beach, South Carolina, and love traveling. Scott is a proud veteran, having served sixteen years in the military between the army and air force reserves.

www.ingramcontent.com/pod-product-compliance
Lightning Source LLC
Chambersburg PA
CBHW071714210326
41597CB00017B/2481